THE NEW FIRST AID IN ENGLISH

REVISED EDITION

BY

ANGUS MACIVER

ISBN 0 7169 4409 x

D1369024

ROBERT GIBSON · Publisher
17 Fitzroy Place, Glasgow, G3 7SF

Contents

		Page
SENTENCES:		
Simple to Complex		104
Complex to Simple		105
ALPHABETICAL ORDER		106
THE APOSTROPHE		107
THE APOSTROPHE AS AN ABBREVIATION		108
CAPITAL LETTERS		109
PUNCTUATION		110
DIMINUTIVES		110
SMALL QUANTITIES		111
FOR REFERENCE (To Find: Look at)		111
PROVERBS		112
COLLOQUIALISMS		115
GENERAL COLLOQUIAL EXPRESSIONS		116
POPULAR PHRASES		118
DOUBLES		119
COLOURS		120
OUR FIVE SENSES		121
DERIVATIONS:		
Roots		122
Prefixes		123
Suffixes		124
GENERAL KNOWLEDGE		125
FASTENINGS		131
USEFUL INFORMATION		132
Countries, Peoples, Languages		133
Place Names		134
Countries, Capitals, Currencies		136
Do You Know?		137
The Wonders of the World		138
Science		140
SPELLING LISTS		141
GENERAL TESTS		145
TESTS IN COMPREHENSION		167
PRONUNCIATION AND SPELLING		179
PHRASAL VERBS		192

PARTS OF SPEECH

THE ENGLISH LANGUAGE is now spoken in many parts of the world and owes its widespread use to the fact that it is one of the most progressive of modern languages. The language was first spoken by various tribes in Denmark and Northern Germany and was introduced into this country when they settled here in the fifth and sixth centuries.

The majority of words in English are of this Anglo-Saxon origin but, with the progress of civilisation and continuous contact with other countries, many words are now in common use which have their origin in such languages as Latin, Greek, Celtic, French, Dutch and German.

The words of our language are classified as Parts of Speech and are named according to their functions. This means that every word, dependent on its use, falls into one of the following divisions:

The Noun.
A noun is the name of a person, animal, place or thing, e.g. John, tiger, school, kettle, honesty.

The Verb.
A verb may be said to be a "doing" word, e.g. eat, think, write.

The Pronoun.
A pronoun is a word which takes the place of a noun, e.g. he, she, it.

The Adjective.
An adjective describes a noun or a pronoun, e.g. good, fine, proud.

The Adverb.
An adverb generally modifies a verb, e.g. quietly, here, suddenly.

The Preposition.
A preposition shows the relation between one thing and another, e.g. against, for, with.

The Conjunction.
A conjunction is a word used for joining words and clauses, e.g. and, but.

The Exclamation or Interjection.
An exclamation or interjection expresses sudden emotion, e.g. Oh! Hullo! Stop!

When we wish to express a thought we use words grouped together in a certain order so that we convey a sensible, definite meaning. This combination of words is termed a sentence. In conversation or writing, sentences should always be used in order that the hearer or reader may clearly understand the meaning.

NUMBER

Most nouns have a Singular form used to denote ONE person or thing and a different Plural form denoting MORE than ONE. Pronouns and verbs also have different singular and plural forms.

Singular	Plural	Singular	Plural
box	boxes	child	children
brush	brushes	foot	feet
fox	foxes	goose	geese
gas	gases	man	men
glass	glasses	mouse	mice
watch	watches	ox	oxen
army	armies	tooth	teeth
city	cities	woman	women
fly	flies		
lady	ladies	brother	{ brothers, brethren }
calf	calves		
half	halves	cloth	{ cloths, clothes }
knife	knives		
leaf	leaves	die	{ dies, dice }
life	lives		
loaf	loaves	fish	{ fishes, fish }
shelf	shelves		
thief	thieves	genius	{ geniuses, genii }
wolf	wolves		
chief	chiefs	pea	{ peas, pease }
dwarf	dwarfs		
hoof	hoofs, hooves	penny	{ pennies, pence }
reef	reefs		
roof	roofs	shot	{ shots, shot }
cargo	cargoes		
echo	echoes		
hero	heroes	cannon	cannon
Negro	Negroes	cod	cod
potato	potatoes	deer	deer
banjo	banjos	dozen	dozen
day	days	grouse	grouse
halo	halos	salmon	salmon
piano	pianos	sheep	sheep
solo	solos	swine	swine
valley	valleys	trout	trout

Number

Singular	Plural	Singular	Plural
brother-in-law	brothers-in-law	bye-law	bye-laws
by-way	by-ways	coat-of-mail	coats-of-mail
cupful	cupfuls	mouse-trap	mouse-traps
hanger-on	hangers-on	passer-by	passers-by
maid-of-honour	maids-of-honour	son-in-law	sons-in-law
man-of-war	men-of-war	spoonful	spoonfuls

The following words have no singular:

bellows, billiards, gallows, measles, pincers, pliers, scissors, shears, spectacles, thanks, tidings, tongs, trousers, tweezers, victuals.

EXERCISES

1. State the plural of:

    loaf, man-of-war, piano, sheep, foot, echo, penny, life, deer, ox.

2. Give the singular of:

    ladies, thieves, geese, clothes, trout, passers-by, mice, knives, teeth, boxes.

3. Fill in the blank spaces — the singular or plural form — as required:

army	....	son-in-law	....
....	roofs	cargo	....
....	women	....	children
cupful	....	....	flies
swine	....	halo	....
dwarf	....	....	potatoes

4. Give the plural of:

    police-constable, daughter-in-law, step-child, looker-on, page-boy, washer-woman, housewife, fireman.

5. Give the singular of:

    glasses, hoofs, heroes, feet, pence, fish, shelves, cities, men, leaves.

Number

6. Change all **Singulars** into **Plurals**.

(1) I heard the echo in the cave.
(2) The lady spoke to the child.
(3) The boy went for a loaf.
(4) The man fed the calf.
(5) The mouse ran into a hole.
(6) The knife was lying on the table.
(7) The fisherman caught a trout.
(8) The dwarf gave him a stick.
(9) The ship struck the reef.
(10) My foot troubled me.
(11) It was a man's boot.
(12) The burglar tried to rob my shop.
(13) The prisoner says that he is innocent.
(14) The girl's hat was on the peg.
(15) The boy robbed a bird's nest.
(16) His tooth hurt him badly.
(17) The farmer ploughs his field.
(18) The horse is eating a raw carrot.
(19) The child cried because he was tired.
(20) This is the house in which I stay.

7. Change all **Singulars** into **Plurals** and **Verbs** into the **Past Tense**.

(1) The rabbit runs from the dog.
(2) The girl wears a blue dress.
(3) The sailor swims to his ship.
(4) The woman catches the goose.
(5) The man shoots the deer.
(6) The ox eats the potato.
(7) The lady prefers the rose.
(8) The sheep runs in the valley.
(9) Her foot is badly cut.
(10) The thief steals the valuable bag.
(11) The child runs to the table.
(12) He is a man of means.
(13) I keep the bird in a cage.
(14) He writes my name.
(15) She tells me so.
(16) He has a sharp knife.
(17) She takes his pencil.
(18) The old woman sits on that seat.
(19) The man walks slowly to his job.
(20) The mouse scampers from the cat.

8

GENDER

Nouns and pronouns belong to one or another of four GENDERS in grammar. These are:

1.   **MASCULINE** — words denoting male creatures, e.g. **boy, king.**
2.   **FEMININE** — words denoting female creatures, e.g. **girl, queen.**
3.   **COMMON** — words denoting creatures of either sex, e.g. **child, owner.**
4.   **NEUTER** — words denoting things of neither sex, e.g. **house, box.**

Masculine	Feminine	Masculine	Feminine
abbot	abbess	bachelor	spinster
actor	actress	beau	belle
author	authoress	boy	girl
baron	baroness	brave	squaw
conductor	conductress	bridegroom	bride
count	countess	brother	sister
deacon	deaconess	Czar	Czarina
duke	duchess	don	donna
emperor	empress	earl	countess
enchanter	enchantress	executor	executrix
giant	giantess	father	mother
god	goddess	fiancé	fiancée
heir	heiress	friar	nun
host	hostess	gentleman	lady
hunter	huntress	governor	matron
instructor	instructress	he	she
Jew	Jewess	hero	heroine
lion	lioness	him	her
manager	manageress	husband	wife
marquis	marchioness	king	queen
master	mistress	lad	lass
mayor	mayoress	lord	lady
murderer	murderess	male	female
negro	negress	man	woman
ogre	ogress	masseur	masseuse
patron	patroness	monk	nun
peer	peeress	Mr.	Mrs.
poet	poetess	nephew	niece
priest	priestess	papa	mama
prince	princess	proprietor	proprietrix

Gender

Masculine	Feminine	Masculine	Feminine
prophet	prophetess	sir	madam
shepherd	shepherdess	sloven	slut
sorcerer	sorceress	son	daughter
steward	stewardess	Sultan	Sultana
tailor	tailoress	tutor	governess
tiger	tigress	uncle	aunt
traitor	traitress	widower	widow
waiter	waitress	wizard	witch

Masculine	Feminine	Masculine	Feminine
boar	sow	Billy-goat	Nanny-goat
buck	doe	buck-rabbit	doe-rabbit
bull	cow	bull-calf	cow-calf
bullock	heifer	Boy Scout	Girl Guide
cock	hen	cock-sparrow	hen-sparrow
colt	filly	father-in-law	mother-in-law
cob (swan)	pen	grandfather	grandmother
dog	bitch	headmaster	headmistress
drake	duck	he-goat	she-goat
gander	goose	Jack-ass	Jenny-ass
hart	hind	landlord	landlady
hold (ferret)	jill	male-child	female-child
hound	brach	manservant	maidservant
mallard	wild-duck	postman	postwoman
ram	ewe	postmaster	postmistress
sire	dam	son-in-law	daughter-in-law
stag	hind	step-father	step-mother
stallion	mare	step-son	step-daughter
steer	heifer		

Masculine	Feminine	Masculine	Feminine
Alexander	Alexandra	John	Joan
Cecil	Cecilia	Joseph	Josephine
Charles	Charlotte	Oliver	Olive
Christian	Christina	Patrick	Patricia
Clarence	Clara	Paul	Pauline
Francis	Frances	Robert	Roberta
George	Georgina	Victor	Victoria
Henry	Henrietta	William	Wilhelmina

Gender

COMMON GENDER words denote creatures of **either sex** and the same word may be used **both of male and of female,** e.g.

> adult, animal, baby, bird, cat, cattle, child, companion, comrade, cousin, darling, dear, deer, fowl, friend, guardian, guest, infant, juvenile, orphan, owner, parent, passenger, pig, pupil, relation, relative, scholar, sheep, singer, swan, teacher, tourist, traveller, visitor.

NEUTER GENDER words denote **things without life or sex,** e.g.

> bag, boots, box, bread, butter, chair, chalk, chimney, church, cocoa, coffee, desk, dishes, door, floor, house, jacket, jotter, kettle, knife, mirror, pencil, pillow, ruler, school, seat, stairs, street, table.

Exceptions

We often speak of lifeless things as being male or female, e.g.

> A sailor refers to his ship as **she.**
> An engine-driver refers to his engine as **she.**
> A motorist refers to his car as **she.**
> An aviator refers to his aeroplane as **she.**

Names of things that suggest **power** or **dignity** are spoken of as if they were **masculine,** e.g.

> Time, Winter, Mountains, Sun, Death.

Names of things that suggest **beauty** or **gentleness** are spoken of as if they were **feminine,** e.g.

> Spring, Moon, Liberty, Peace, Nature.

On the other hand, we sometimes refer to a cat, dog, horse and even a child as **it.**

EXERCISES

1. Give the feminine of:

> heir, monk, stallion, nephew, gander, waiter, sir, ram, hero, bachelor.

2. Give the masculine of:

> witch, filly, cow, maidservant, wife, duck, bride, vixen, duchess, aunt.

Gender

3. State the gender of:

lion, cousin, jotter, mistress, friend, pencil, steward, sister, book, child.

4. Give the feminine of:

headmaster, step-father, son-in-law, Boy Scout, Billy-goat.

5. Fill in blank spaces — the masculine or feminine form — as required:

lion	....	bull	....
....	lady	grandfather	....
....	governess	....	hind
male	....	....	widow
actor	....	tom-cat	....
tailor	....	....	slut

6. Give the corresponding feminine of:

Joseph, Henry, Patrick, Charles, John.

7. Change all **Masculines** into corresponding **Feminines**:

(1) The bridegroom is my nephew.
(2) The instructor ordered him to jump.
(3) My landlord is a widower.
(4) The wizard spoke to the prince.
(5) The bull attacked the milkman.
(6) The Duke chatted to the man.
(7) The heir to the estate is a bachelor.
(8) "No, sir," he replied.
(9) The waiter served his own brother.
(10) "He was indeed a hero," said the emperor.
(11) The lion sprang at the colt.
(12) The master gave instructions to the manservant.
(13) "Well!" said his grandfather, "How are you, my little lad?"
(14) The steward brought a glass of water to my uncle, who was seasick.
(15) The conductor of the car directed the famous actor to the theatre.
(16) The proprietor of the hotel was a wealthy earl.
(17) The host was extremely puzzled by the twin brothers.
(18) The son of a king is termed a prince.
(19) The mayor talked to the father of the little boy.

(20) The old man told his shepherd to search for the ram.
(21) His father-in-law spoke to the manager.
(22) He was the step-son of an elderly count.
(23) The headmaster rebuked the boy for his conduct.
(24) Henry has a brother who is a Boy Scout.
(25) The Negro owned a pet gander called Joseph.

FAMILIES

Parents		Young
father	mother	baby or child
king	queen	prince or princess
man	woman	baby or child
Red Indian	squaw	papoose
uncle	aunt	nephew or niece
bear	she-bear	cub
Billy-goat	Nanny-goat	kid
boar (pig)	sow	porkling, piglet
buck (deer)	hind	fawn
buck (hare)	doe	leveret
buck (rabbit)	doe	rack
bull (cattle)	cow	calf
bull (elephant)	cow	calf
bull (seal)	cow	calf
bull (whale)	cow	calf
cob (swan)	pen	cygnet
cock (fowl)	hen	chicken
cock (pigeon)	hen	squab
dog	bitch	pup
dog (fox)	vixen	cub
drake	duck	duckling
eagle	eagle	eaglet
gander	goose	gosling
hawk	bowess	bowet
hold (ferret)	jill	hob
leopard	leopardess	cub
lion	lioness	cub

Gender

Parents		Young
owl	owl	owlet
ram (sheep)	ewe	lamb
stag (Red Deer)	hind	fawn
stallion	mare	foal
tiercel (peregrine)	falcon	eyas
tiger	tigress	cub
tom-cat	queen or tabby-cat	kitten
wolf	she-wolf	cub

Adult	Young	Adult	Young
bee	grub	moth	caterpillar
bird	nestling	salmon	parr
butterfly	caterpillar	toad	tadpole
eel	elver	trout	fry
frog	tadpole	wasp	grub

EXERCISES

1. Name the young of:

    fox, eagle, goose, sheep, pig, goat, cow, horse.

2. Name the parent of:

    fawn, pup, cygnet, chicken, leveret, kitten, owlet, duckling.

3. Fill in the blank spaces — the name of parent or young — as required:

wolf	....	....	kid
....	foal	bear	....
sow	....	....	lamb
....	gosling	eagle	....

4. Give the names for:

    a young salmon, a young eel, a young cod, a young trout, a young bird.

14

TRADITIONAL HOMES

Person	Home	Creature	Home
Arab	dowar	ape	tree-nest
Aborigine	humpy	badger	sett, earth
convict	prison	bear	den
Eskimo	igloo	beaver	lodge
gipsy	caravan	bee	hive
king	palace	bird	nest
lumberman	log-cabin	cow	byre
man	house	dog	kennel
Maori	whare	eagle	eyrie
minister	manse	fowl	coop
monk	monastery	fox	earth, lair
noble	castle	hare	form
nun	convent	horse	stable
parson	parsonage	lion	lair, den
pioneer	wagon	mole	fortress
priest (eastern)	temple	mouse	hole, nest
prisoner	cell	otter	holt
Red Indian	wigwam	owl	barn, tree
Red Indian	tepee	pig	sty
soldier	barracks	pigeon	dove-cote
soldier	camp	rabbit (tame)	hutch
Swiss (herdsman)	chalet	rabbit (wild)	burrow, warren
tinker	tent	sheep	pen, fold
vicar	vicarage	snail	shell
Zulu	kraal	spider	web
		squirrel	drey
		tiger	lair
		wasp	nest, vespiary

EXERCISES

1. Name the homes of:
   peasant, king, minister, lumberman, parson, monk, Red Indian, Arab, Eskimo, Zulu.

2. Whom would you expect to find living in the following?
   convent, palace, barracks, cell, vicarage.

3. Name the homes of the following creatures:
   cow, dog, eagle, bee, pig, fox, wild rabbit, wasp, bird, lion.

4. What creatures live in the following places?
   dove-cot, hutch, pen, form, stable.

NAMES

First or Christian or Given Names: names given to children at their christening or baptism, usually different for boys and girls. Many are names of Biblical characters and ancient heroes and heroines. Most have shortened forms — so-called 'pet' names.

Male	Female
Albert (Bert, Bertie)	Agnes (Aggie, Nessie, Senga)
Alexander (Alick, Sandy)	Alice (Elsie)
Alfred (Alf)	Amanda (Mandy)
Andrew (Andy, Drew)	Angela (Angie)
Anthony (Tony)	Ann (Annie, Nan, Nancy)
Archibald (Archie, Baldy)	Barbara (Babs, Babbie)
Brian	Catherine (Cathie, Kate, Kitty)
Charles (Charlie)	Cecilia (Cis, Cissie)
Christopher (Chris, Kit)	Christina (Chrissie, Tina)
Daniel (Dan, Danny)	Diana (Di)
David (Dave)	Dorothy (Dot, Dolly)
Edward (Ed, Ned, Ted)	Eleanor (Ella, Nell, Nora)
Francis (Frank)	Elizabeth (Bessie, Betty, Lizzie)
Frederick (Fred, Freddy)	Fiona
George (Geordie, Dod)	Florence (Flo, Flossie)
Gordon	Grace
Henry (Harry, Hal)	Heather
Hugh (Hughie)	Helen (Nell, Nellie)
James (Jem, Jim, Jimmy)	Isobel (Isa, Bella, Tibbie)
John (Johnny, Jack, Jock)	Jane (Jean, Jeanie)
Joseph (Joe, Joey)	Janet (Jenny, Jess, Jessie)
Laurence (Larry)	Judith (Judy)
Michael (Mike, Micky)	Julia (Julie)
Nigel	Lilian (Lily)
Oliver (Nol, Nolly)	Margaret (Marjory, Maggie, Peggy)
Patrick (Pat, Paddy)	Marion (Mamie)
Peter (Pete, Peterkin)	Mary (May, Molly, Polly)
Philip (Phil)	Rebecca (Beck, Becky)
Richard (Dick, Dicky)	Rose (Rosie)
Robert (Bob, Bobby, Robin, Bert)	Sarah (Sally, Sadie)
Samuel (Sam, Sammy)	Susan (Sue, Susie)
Stephen (Steve)	Victoria (Vicky)
Thomas (Tom, Tommy)	Violet (Vi)
Walter (Wat)	Yvonne
William (Bill, Will, Willie)	Zoé

Many first names have a meaning in Hebrew, Greek or Latin, e.g. Amanda — lovable; Catherine — pure; Charles — manly; Christopher — carrier of Christ; Clement — merciful; Cyril — lordly; Donald — world chief; Ethel — noble; Fiona — fair; Hilary — cheerful; Margaret — pearl; Peter — rock; Philip — lover of horses; Stephen — crown; Thomas — twin; Zoé — life.

Surnames: a child's last name is the family name of the child's father. On marriage a woman normally takes the surname of her husband, though nowadays some do not. Note, however, that in China the surname is not the last, but the first name (see below).

Surnames are derived from many sources such as Christian names, occupations, places, animals, birds, colours and qualities of mind or body.

From Christian names: Archibald, Charles, Francis, Patrick.

A great many surnames are composed of a Christian name and a form of the word "son of" added, e.g. Adamson, Davidson, Donaldson, Neilson, Richardson, Williamson.

In England and Ireland "son of" is sometimes shown by **Fitz**, e.g. Fitzgerald, Fitzpatrick, Fitzwilliam.

In Wales **"ap"** or **"ab"** (in each case small letters) denotes "son of", e.g. Dafydd ab Edmund — David son of Edmund. The surnames Upjohn and Uprichard are still used. It became the custom to cut short the **"ab"** or **"ap"** to a simple **"b"** or **"p"** and thus the following surnames appeared: Bellis, Broderick, Parry, Pritchard. Later many Welsh surnames were formed by adding an **"s"** to Christian names, e.g. Davies, Hughes, Jones, Phillips, Roberts, Williams.

In the Highlands of Scotland **Mac** (son of) is very common, e.g. MacArthur, MacDonald, MacDougall, MacGregor, MacNeil, MacWilliam. In some cases the second part of such names is not spelt with a capital letter. In these cases this part of the name is not itself a Christian name like Arthur or William, e.g. Macnab — son of the abbot; Macintyre — son of the carpenter; Mackintosh — son of the Thane; Macpherson — son of the parson.

In Ireland "son of" is generally shown by **Mc**, e.g. McAdam, McDonald, McNeil, McWilliam.

It is interesting to note that at one time in Ireland the head of a family was the grandfather, who had his children and his children's children about him, just as with the Israelites of Bible days. This caused **O'** (from Ogha, meaning "grandson of") to appear in surnames, e.g. O'Brien, O'Connor, O'Donnell, O'Neil.

Names

In other countries also some names denote "son of" (see below).

Many surnames were formed as shown below:

From **Occupations:** Archer, Baker, Clark, Cook, Farmer, Fisher, Hunter, Mason, Miller, Porter, Shepherd, Slater, Smith, Taylor, Wright.

From **Places:** Burns, Cape, England, Forest, Ford, Hall, Hamilton, Hill, Lake, London, Mills, Scotland, Stirling, Wells, Woods.

From **Animals:** Bullock, Fox, Hare, Hart, Hogg, Lamb, Lyon, Wolfe.

From **Birds:** Drake, Nightingale, Peacock, Swan, Wren.

From **Colours:** Black, Blue, Brown, Gray, Green, White.

From **Qualities of Mind or Body:** Blyth, Bright, Gay, Good, Hardie, Little, Merry, Noble, Short, Small, Smart, Strong, Young.

Names in other countries.

In Kenya the word **"arap"** in a name means son of, e.g. the respected President of Kenya is named Daniel Toroitich arap Moi. Similarly in other districts the Kikuyu, Kamba, Meru and Embu tribes use **"wa"** meaning son of or daughter of.

In Malaysia many names show an Arabic origin indicating the son or daughter status by the use of **"bin"** (boy) or **"binte"** (girl), e.g. Achmed bin Faued or Faridah binte Hussein.

In Singapore Indian names would include S/O (Son of) or D/O (Daughter of), e.g. Selvarajoo S/O Velu or Saraswethy D/O Rajoo.

In China names are written with the family name first, e.g. the Prime Minister of Singapore is the Honourable Lee Kuan Yew, Lee being the family name. An interesting fact about Chinese names is that the second name denotes the generation. As an example take the name Tan Wu Cheng. Tan is the family name, Wu the generation name and Cheng the personal name. Should Mr. Tan have a brother or brothers they will all bear the same family name, Tan, followed by the generation name Wu followed by their own personal name, Cheng or Ling or any other given name.

In Iceland the boy or girl would, in addition to their own personal name, be given their father's name with the addition of son or daughter, e.g. Magnus' father was called John so Magnus Johnson would be the boy's name.

GROUP TERMS OR COLLECTIONS

ANIMATE

an army of soldiers
a band of musicians
à bench of bishops
a bench of magistrates
a bevy of ladies
a board of directors
a brood of chickens
a building of rooks
a choir of singers
a class of scholars
a company of actors
a covey of grouse
a crew of sailors
a drove of cattle
a flock of birds
a flock of sheep
a gaggle of geese
a gang of labourers
a gang of thieves
a herd of buffaloes
a herd of cattle
a host of angels

a litter of cubs
a litter of pups
a nest of rabbits
a pack of rascals
a pack of wolves
a plague of insects
a plague of locusts
a pride of lions
a school of whales
a shoal of herring
a staff of servants
a staff of teachers
a stud of horses
a swarm of bees
a swarm of insects
a team of horses
a team of oxen
a team of players
a tribe of natives
a troop of monkeys
a troupe of dancers
a troupe of minstrels

INANIMATE

a bale of cotton, wool
a batch of bread
a bouquet of flowers
a bunch of grapes
a bundle of rags
a chest of drawers
a clump of trees
a cluster of diamonds, stars
a clutch of eggs
a collection of pictures
a crate of fruit
a fleet of motor cars, ships
a flight of aeroplanes, steps

a forest of trees
a hail of fire
a hedge of bushes
a library of books
a pack of cards
a rope of pearls
a set of china, clubs, tools
a sheaf of corn
a stack of hay
a string of beads
a suit of clothes
a suite of furniture, rooms
a tuft of grass

Group Terms or Collections

PEOPLE

at a concert	audience
in church	congregation
in the street	crowd, throng
in a riot	mob
in a rowdy scene	rabble

Less Common Examples

a baren of mules

a bevy of quails

a cast of hawks

a cete of badgers

a clowder of cats

a coffle of slaves

a covert of coots

a down of hares

a fall of woodcocks

a field of runners

a flight of doves

a flight of swallows

a gang of elks

a gathering of clans

a herd of antelopes

a herd of cranes

a host of sparrows

a kindle of kittens

a labour of moles

a leap of leopards

a muster of peacocks

a nest of mice

a nide of pheasants

a pace of asses

a paddling of ducks

a posse of sheriff's men

a rag of colts

a siege of herons

a skulk of foxes

a sloth of bears

a smuck of jellyfish

a stand of plovers

a string of horses

a tribe of goats

a watch of nightingales

a wisp of snipe

———

a budget of papers

a cast of flower-pots

a crate of crockery

a fusillade of shots

a galaxy of stars

a group of islands

a bunch of bananas

a nest of machine-guns

a peal of bells

a punnet of strawberries

a sheaf of arrows

a shock of wheat

a skein of silk

a skein of wool

a truss of hay

Group Terms or Collections

1. A number of sheep together is called a **flock**. What name is given to a number of:

   singers, ships, wolves, trees, savages, bees, whales, thieves, players, pups?

2. Of what are these collections?

   menagerie, mob, regiment, bundle, heap.

3. Supply the missing word:

   a .... of motor cars   a .... of herring

   a .... of servants   a .... of cattle

   a .... of angels   a .... of directors

   a .... of grapes   a .... of chickens

   a .... of monkeys   a .... of books

4. Insert the most suitable word in each of the following:

   a litter of ....   a cluster of ....

   a band of ....   a stack of ....

   a building of ....   a party of ....

   a plague of ....   a crew of ....

   a bouquet of ....   an army of ....

5. Give one word for a number of people:

   (1) at a concert;   (4) in a riot;

   (2) in church;   (5) in a rowdy scene;

   (3) in the street;   (6) at a football match.

6. The following words represent a definite number:

   single, couple, brace, pair, dozen, score, gross.

   Place the words in the phrases best suited to their use:

   a .... eggs   a .... of boots

   a .... of pencils   a .... ticket

   a .... of sheep   a .... of grouse

            a .... of chairs

7. At my uncle's farm I saw:

   a .... of sheep   a .... of cattle

   a .... of pups   a .... of chickens

   a .... of bees   a .... of geese

Group Terms or Collections

8. Insert the most suitable words in the following sentences:

   (1) He was greeted at the station by a .... of friends.

   (2) A .... of thieves had broken into the premises.

   (3) The old shepherd carefully counted his .... of sheep.

   (4) An .... of ants moved slowly across our path.

   (5) The fishermen saw signs of the presence of a .... of herring.

   (6) At the evening service, the minister preached to a large ....

   (7) The attackers were met by a .... of fire.

   (8) His whole .... of cattle had been affected by the drought.

   (9) The travellers were hotly pursued by a .... of wolves.

  (10) He attended a meeting of the .... of directors.

9. The following definitions represent **numeral** words; for example, an aeroplane with *one* set of wings is called a **monoplane**. How many can you recognize and properly name?

   (1) One person singing.

   (2) A single eye-glass.

   (3) A fabled animal with one horn.

   (4) A two-wheeled cycle.

   (5) A two-footed animal.

   (6) An aeroplane with two sets of wings.

   (7) Two persons singing together.

   (8) Two babies born at the same time.

   (9) A combat between two people.

  (10) A three-legged stand or support.

  (11) Three persons singing together.

  (12) An aeroplane with three sets of wings.

  (13) A three-wheeled cycle.

  (14) A four-footed animal.

  (15) Four persons singing together.

  (16) A period of ten years.

  (17) A period of a hundred years.

  (18) A person aged one hundred years.

  (19) A Roman commander of one hundred men.

  (20) Creatures said to have one hundred feet.

SIMILES compare things which are alike in some respect, although they may be different in their general nature.

1. **Similes showing distinctive qualities of creatures:**

as agile as a monkey
as blind as a bat
as brave as a lion
as bright as a lark
as busy as an ant
as busy as a bee
as calm as a cat
as crafty as a fox
as cunning as a fox
as devoted as a mother
as fast as a deer
as fast as a hare
as fat as a pig
as feeble as a child
as fierce as a lion
as flat as a flounder
as fleet as a gazelle
as frisky as a lamb
as frisky as a two-year-old
as gentle as a dove
as gentle as a lamb
as graceful as a swan
as hairy as a gorilla
as happy as a king
as happy as a lark
as happy as a sandboy
as harmless as a dove
as heavy as an elephant
as hungry as a hunter
as hungry as a wolf
as industrious as a beaver
as like as two herring
as loyal as an apostle
as mad as a hatter
as mad as a March hare

as meek as a lamb
as obstinate as a mule
as old as Methuselah
as patient as Job
as playful as a kitten
as playful as a puppy
as pleased as Punch
as plump as a partridge
as poor as a church mouse
as proud as a peacock
as quiet as a mouse
as red as a turkey-cock
as sick as a dog
as silly as a sheep
as slippery as an eel
as slow as a snail
as slow as a tortoise
as sober as a judge
as stolid as a cow
as strong as a horse
as strong as an ox
as sure-footed as a goat
as swift as a deer
as swift as a hare
as swift as a hawk
as tall as a giant
as tenacious as a bulldog
as tender as a chicken
as tender as a shepherd
as thick as thieves
as timid as a mouse
as timid as a rabbit
as wise as an owl
as wise as Solomon
as white as a ghost

Similes

2. **Similes showing special qualities of things:**

as bitter as gall
as black as coal
as black as soot
as bold as brass
as bright as a button
as brittle as glass
as brown as a berry
as clean as a whistle
as clear as a bell
as clear as crystal
as cold as ice
as cool as a cucumber
as dead as a doornail
as deaf as a doorpost
as dry as a bone
as dull as dishwater
as fat as butter
as fit as a fiddle
as flat as a pancake
as fresh as a daisy
as fresh as paint
as good as gold
as green as grass
as hard as horn
as hard as iron
as hard as nails
as heavy as lead
as hot as a furnace
as keen as mustard
as light as a feather
as like as two peas
as neat as a new pin
as old as the hills
as plain as a pikestaff
as purple as the heather
as quick as lightning
as regular as the clock

as right as rain
as round as a barrel
as round as an orange
as safe as houses
as safe as the bank
as sharp as a needle
as sharp as a razor
as silent as the grave
as smooth as glass
as smooth as velvet
as soft as butter
as soft as down
as soft as putty
as sound as a bell
as sour as vinegar
as steady as a rock
as stiff as a poker
as straight as an arrow
as straight as a ramrod
as sturdy as an oak
as sweet as honey
as thin as a rake
as tough as leather
as true as gospel
as true as steel
as warm as wool
as weak as water
as white as a sheet
as white as snow
as ugly as sin
as changeable as the weather
as cold as charity
as easy as A.B.C.
as easy as winking
as large as life
as open as day
as pale as death

EXERCISES

1. We say "As black as coal". Supply the missing words in the following:

    As sharp as   ....   As slippery as ....
    As meek as   ....   As keen as   ....
    As brave as   ....   As swift as   ....
    As sweet as   ....   As clear as   ....
    As cold as   ....   As light as   ....

2. Complete the following:

    As .... as a monkey   As .... as a rock
    As .... as a flounder   As .... as iron
    As .... as Punch   As .... as a new pin
    As .... as a chicken   As .... as a rabbit
    As .... as a bee   As .... as the hills

3. Complete the following sentences with suitable words:

    (1) The coward was trembling like a ....
    (2) His hands were as cold as ....
    (3) The man could swim like a ....
    (4) The baby was as good as ....
    (5) The boy ran like the ....

4. Pick out (by underlining) the best simile in the following:

    Example: As dry as (a tree, an egg, a bone, an apple).

    (1) As flat as (a kettle, a pancake, a loaf, a saucer).
    (2) As steady as (a rock, a book, a box, a table).
    (3) As fast as (a child, a tortoise, a herring, a deer).
    (4) As proud as (a lamb, a daisy, a peacock, a rabbit).
    (5) As happy as (a giraffe, a lark, a lobster, a serpent).

5. Add what you consider the most suitable word:

    (1) The lake shone like a ....
    (2) The smooth sea was like ....
    (3) The water was clear like ....
    (4) The boy climbed the tree like a ....
    (5) His terrified companion stuck to him like a ....

OCCUPATIONS

Describe in a sentence the occupations of the following:

artist	decorator	journalist	postman
athlete	dentist	judge	reporter
aviator	detective	lawyer	saddler
barber	doctor	locksmith	sailor
blacksmith	draper	magistrate	sawyer
butcher	drover	mason	sculptor
cabinet-maker	engineer	matron	seamstress
caddie	explorer	mechanic	shepherd
caretaker	farmer	milliner	slater
carpenter	farrier	miner	soldier
cashier	florist	minister	stationer
chauffeur	fruiterer	navvy	steeplejack
chemist	gamekeeper	newsagent	stoker
clothier	glazier	nurse	surgeon
clown	governess	optician	tailor
coastguard	greengrocer	pedlar	teacher
cobbler	grocer	physician	tinker
commercial	hairdresser	plumber	tinsmith
traveller	ironmonger	poacher	tourist
conductor	jockey	policeman	witness
confectioner	joiner	porter	wright

With whom do you associate the following?

anvil	gun	plane	shovel
awl	handcuffs	plough	solder
barrow	harness	prescription	spanner
baton	hats	pulpit	spectacles
brief-case	joy-stick	razor	telescope
cart	knife	rifle	thimble
cleaver	lancet	roofs	ticket-punch
forceps	mail	safety-lamp	tins
furnace	oath	saw	trumpet
glasscutter	pack	scales	ward
guide-book	palette	sheep	wig

Name the chief persons connected with the following:

army	hospital	Police Station	school
church	navy	Post Office	ship
college	newspaper	prison	Sunday Scho
committee	orchestra	railway station	team of play
court of law	Parliament	Salvation Army	workshop

26

EXERCISES

1. **What am I called?**
   (1) I build stone houses.
   (2) I carry bags at the railway station.
   (3) I write stories for newspapers.
   (4) I ride horses in races.
   (5) I am learning a trade.

2. Many shopkeepers draw attention to their places of business by hanging special signs above their shop-doors. What special sign is displayed by

   (1) a bootmaker;   (4) a hairdresser;   (7) a pawnbroker;
   (2) a chemist;   (5) a locksmith;   (8) a saddler;
   (3) a fishmonger;   (6) an optician;   (9) a watchmaker?

3. In each of the following give one word for a person who

   (1) attends to people's teeth;   (7) looks after people's eyes;
   (2) carves in stone;   (8) mends pots and pans;
   (3) searches for new lands;   (9) repairs boots and shoes;
   (4) draws plans for buildings;   (10) sells from door to door;
   (5) flies an aeroplane;   (11) studies the stars;
   (6) investigates crime;   (12) conducts sales by bidding.

4. Arrange the following as you see them advertised in shop windows:
   best assorted, good fresh, fine ripe, splendid cooking, sweet juicy, young spring.

   apples, chocolates, herring, onions, oranges, tomatoes.

THE HEART'S DESIRE

Beauty says the **Artist.**
Sport says the **Athlete.**
Kindness says the **Child.**
Healing says the **Doctor.**
Power says the **Engineer.**
Abundance says the **Farmer.**
Pleasure says the **Fool.**
Food says the **Glutton.**
Love says the **Maiden.**

Commerce says the **Merchant.**
Gold says the **Miser.**
Home says the **Mother.**
Order says the **Policeman.**
Truth says the **Sage.**
Honour says the **Soldier.**
Fame says the **Statesman.**
Knowledge says the **Student.**
Rest says the **Toiler.**

PLACES

Worship

Abbey, cathedral, chapel, church, convent, kirk, monastery, mosque, pagoda, priory, synagogue, tabernacle, temple.

Business

What are the places called where the following are made?

beer, bread, films, flour, iron goods, leather, money, paper, ships, whisky.

Name particular places where the following are sold:

bread, clothes, dresses, fish, flowers, fruit, general foodstuffs, hats, meat, milk, newspapers, poultry, spectacles, stockings, sweetmeats, tobacco, vegetables, writing materials.

Sport

Give particular names of the places where the following are played:

badminton, bowls, boxing, cricket, croquet, football, golf, hockey, putting, rugby, running, skating, sleighing, tennis, wrestling.

General

Give the particular names of the places connected with the following:

Where

aeroplanes are kept
bees are kept
birds are kept
bull-fighting is held
chickens are hatched
cooks prepare food
criminals are kept
crows build their nests
doctors receive their patients
films are shown
fish are kept
fruit trees grow
gas is stored
grain is stored
grapes are grown

Where

historical relics are shown
law is meted out
motor cars are kept
operations are performed
orphans are kept
people are buried
people lunch for payment
plays are shown
pupils are educated
soldiers are stationed
water is stored
wild animals are kept
young plants and flowers are
  reared
young trees are grown

RECEPTACLES

1. It is interesting to note the types of containers used to hold and carry foodstuffs, e.g.:

> **bag** — cocoa, coffee, rice, sago, sugar.
> **barrel** — apples, herring, oil, potatoes.
> **box** — apples, butter, currants, fish.
> **cask** — butter, mustard.
> **chest** — tea, cloves.
> **sack** — flour, potatoes.

2. Name the contents you would expect to find in the following:

attaché-case	case	handbag	satchel
band-box	cask	hogshead	scabbard
barrel	cellar	jar	scuttle
basin	compact	jug	sheath
basket	creel	keg	still
bath	cruet	kettle	tank
bin	cup	kitbag	tankard
boiler	cupboard	library	tea-pot
bottle	decanter	packet	Thermos flask
bowl	drum	pan	till
box	envelope	phial	trunk
brief-case	ewer	pitcher	tub
bunker	flagon	pocket-book	tumbler
butt	flask	portfolio	tun
caddy	fob	pot	urn
can	gasometer	punnet	vase
canister	goblet	purse	vat
carafe	grip	reticule	wallet
carton	hamper	safe	wardrobe

3. In what receptacles or containers would you expect to find the following?

> **Example:** tea — caddy.

money............	jam	sword ....
water	coal	flowers ....
sauce	hat	arrows ....

SOUNDS AND MOTIONS

All creatures make sounds and move in a fashion peculiar to their species. Their outstanding characteristics are described by the common adjectives.

Creature	Sound	Motion	Common Adjective
ape	gibbers	swings	ungainly
ass	brays	jogs	stupid
bear	growls	lumbers	clumsy
bee	hums	flits	busy
beetle	drones	crawls	horrid
bull	bellows	charges	angry
cat	purrs	steals	sleek
cow	lows	wanders	stolid
deer	bells	bounds	fallow
dog	barks	runs	faithful
donkey	brays	trots	obstinate
elephant	trumpets	ambles	ponderous
frog	croaks	leaps	clammy
horse	neighs	gallops	noble
hound	bays	bounds	gallant
hyena	screams	prowls	cunning
lamb	bleats	frisks	gentle
lion	roars	prowls	tawny
monkey	chatters	climbs	agile
mouse	squeaks	scampers	timid
person	talks	walks	average
pig	grunts	trots	fat
rabbit	squeals	leaps	timid
serpent	hisses	glides	loathsome
wolf	howls	lopes	lean
bird	whistles	flies	swift
cock	crows	struts	proud
crow	caws	flaps	black
curlew	pipes	flits	lonely
duck	quacks	waddles	waddling
eagle	screams	swoops	proud
hen	cackles	struts	domestic
lark	sings	soars	gentle
owl	hoots	flits	tawny

Sounds and Motions

Creature	Sound	Motion	Common Adjective
parrot	screeches	flits	saucy
pigeon	coos	flutters	gentle
robin	chirps	hops	little
seagull	screams	glides	tireless
sparrow	chirps	flits	little
swallow	twitters	dives	swift
turkey	gobbles	struts	plump
wren	warbles	hops	tiny

aquiline	—like an eagle	ferine	—like a wild beast
asinine	—like an ass	leonine	—like a lion
bovine	—like a cow or ox	lupine	—like a wolf
canine	—like a dog	ovine	—like a sheep
corvine	—like a crow	piscine	—like a fish
elephantine	—like an elephant	porcine	—like a pig
equine	—like a horse	tigrine	—like a tiger
feline	—like a cat	vulpine	—like a fox

Certain words are used in **imitation** of the sounds made by creatures, e.g.:

ass	— hee-haw	**duck**	— quack
cat	— me-ow	**hen**	— cluck
cock	— cock-a-doodle-do	**owl**	— tu-whoo
cow	— moo	**rook**	— caw
cuckoo	— cuckoo	**sheep**	— baa
dog	— bow-wow	**sparrow**	— tweet-tweet

The following verbs are obtained from the **habits** of creatures:

to ape	— to imitate foolishly
to badger	— to worry or tease
to crow	— to boast or swagger
to dog	— to follow or track
to duck	— to dip or plunge
to ferret	— to search out
to fox	— to act cunningly
to hound	— to pursue relentlessly
to ram	— to drive or push into
to wolf	— to eat greedily

Sounds and Motions

1. Animals make different sounds, e.g. The dog **barks**.

    What sounds are made by the following animals?
    donkey, elephant, horse, pig, wolf, monkey, deer, cow, bear, hyena.

2. Write the names of the creatures:

    The .... bays.   The .... croaks.
    The .... hisses.   The .... purrs.
    The .... crows.   The .... gobbles.
    The .... bleats.   The .... roars.
    The .... caws.   The .... quacks.

3. Describe the movements of the following, e.g. The horse **gallops**.

    The frog   ....   The duck ....
    The monkey...............   The lamb ....
    The wolf   ....   The lark ....
    The seagull ....   The bear ....

4. Apply the most fitting adjective:

    sleek, cunning, obstinate, fat, tireless, loathsome, gentle, faithful.

    The .... mule.   The .... fox.
    The .... pig.   The .... lamb.
    The .... dog.   The .... cat.
    The .... serpent.   The .... seagull.

5. What is meant by calling a person

    (1) an ape   (8)   a fox   (15) a rabbit
    (2) an ass   (9)   a goat   (16) a sheep
    (3) a bear   (10) a horse   (17) a snail
    (4) a bull   (11) a hound   (18) a swine
    (5) a dog   (12) a lamb   (19) a tortoise
    (6) a donkey   (13) a lion   (20) a viper
    (7) an elephant   (14) a pig   (21) a wolf?

6. "Pussy" is the pet name for a cat. Which creature does each of the following pet names represent?

    Polly, Fido, Dicky, Jumbo, Jacko, Bruin, Bunny, Dobbin, Neddy.

7. Which creatures were the speakers thinking of when they said?

    (1) "The man bellowed with rage."
    (2) "He has the hump today."
    (3) "We were stung by his remarks."
    (4) "Don't crow so loudly."
    (5) "The officer barked an order."
    (6) "The witch spoke in a croaky voice."
    (7) "He grunted in reply."
    (8) "The girls were chattering in the hall."
    (9) "Why are you galloping along the corridor?"
    (10) "The boy howled when he was caught."
    (11) "The wicked old woman cackled loudly as she stirred the pot."
    (12) "The lecturer's voice droned on and on."
    (13) "The little girl screeched with delight."
    (14) "The captain snorted in disgust."
    (15) "The curious child prowled about the room."
    (16) "Loud hooting interrupted the speech."

8. Explain the words underlined in the following sentences:

    (1) He had an <u>aquiline</u> nose.
    (2) The burglar walked with a <u>feline</u> tread.
    (3) The yokel had a <u>bovine</u> look.
    (4) He was scolded for his <u>asinine</u> conduct.
    (5) They had the appearance of sharp <u>canine</u> teeth.

9. What feeling is expressed by

(1)	a chuckle	(5)	a hoot	(9)	a sigh
(2)	a groan	(6)	a howl	(10)	a sniff
(3)	a growl	(7)	a roar	(11)	a snort
(4)	a grunt	(8)	a screech	(12)	a squeal?

10. Complete the following:

    On a recent visit to a large farm I heard various animal sounds. I heard

    a cock ....,   cows ....,   pigs ....,
    ducks ....,   horses ....,   lambs ....,
    turkeys ....   and a dog ....

SOUNDS
Made by Objects

Note that the words have been formed to resemble the sounds made by the objects.

babble of a stream
bang of a door
beat of a drum
blare of a trumpet
blast of an explosion
booming of a gun
bubbling of water
buzz of a saw
call of a bugle
chime of a bell (large)
chime of a clock
chug of an engine
clang of an anvil
clang of a bell
clanking of chains
clatter of hoofs
clink of a coin
crack of a whip
crackling of wood
creak of a hinge
crinkle of paper
dripping of water
grinding of brakes
gurgle of a stream
hissing of steam
hoot of a horn
howling of the wind
jangling of chains
jingle of coins
lapping of water
lash of a whip
murmur of a stream
patter of feet
patter of rain
pealing of bells

ping of a bullet
popping of corks
purr of an engine
rattling of dishes
report of a rifle
ring of metal
ring of a telephone
ringing of bells
roar of a torrent
rumble of a train
rustle of silk
rustling of leaves
scrape of a bow
screeching of brakes
shriek of a whistle
shuffling of feet
sighing of the wind
singing of the kettle
skirl of the bagpipes
slam of a door
splutter of an engine
swish of skirts
tick of a clock
tinkle of a bell (small)
tinkle of glass
throb of an engine
thunder of hoofs
toot of a horn
tramp of feet
twang of a bow
wail of a siren
whack of a cane
whirring of wings
whoosh of a rocket

EXERCISES

1. Insert suitable words in the blank spaces:

> **Example:** The **beat** of a drum.

The .... of a hinge.   The .... of a whip.

The .... of brakes.   The .... of steam.

The .... of feet.   The .... of silk.

The .... of a bugle.   The .... of a clock.

2. Supply the missing words:

> **Example:** The clatter of **hoofs**.

The pealing of ....   The popping of..................

The booming of..................   The skirl of the..................

The crinkle of ....   The throb of an..................

The slam of a ....   The toot of a ....

3. Use the right words in the following:

A boiling kettle .... Thunder .... Frying fat .... in the pan. The rain .... on the window. Coins .... in the bag. I heard the .... of a rifle. The heavy bar fell with a .... Suddenly we heard the .... of hoofs. We were awakened by the .... of the big church clock. The passengers heard the loud .... of brakes. The rude boy .... the door behind him. The north wind .... in the chimney.

4. Complete the following by adding a sentence which indicates the cause of the sound. No. 1 is done for you:

(1) **Toot! Toot!** The sound of a motor-horn warned us of danger.

(2) **Bang!** . . . .

(3) **Boom!** . . . .

(4) **Crash!** . . . .

(5) **Plop!** . . . .

(6) **Rat-tat-tat!** . . . .

(7) **Splash!** . . . .

(8) **Tick-tock!** . . . .

(9) **Ting-a-ling!** . . . .

CLASSIFICATION

All things on earth may be divided into two classes:
    (1)   **Animate** (living things).
    (2)   **Inanimate** (things having no life).

1.   **The animate or living things** consist of creatures and plants. Creatures can eat, grow and move about from place to place, e.g. animals including people, birds, fishes, insects, reptiles. Plants are fixed by means of roots and although they can absorb food and grow they cannot move about from place to place, e.g. trees, flowers, vegetables.

2.   **The inanimate or things having no life** are fixed, cannot eat, cannot grow and cannot move about from place to place, e.g. stone, cloth, knife.

Every object can be placed in a certain general class either because of its resemblance to other things or because of its purpose or use. **The following are general classes:** animals, birds, insects, fishes, reptiles, flowers, fruits, trees, vegetables, minerals, liquids, apparel, occupations, places, utensils, ships, games, vehicles, cereals, coins, instruments.

1.   **Write one name for each of the following groups, e.g.**

        iron, lead, copper, silver: **metals**

    (1) lion, bear, goat, mouse   ....
    (2) jacket, blouse, trousers, skirt   ....
    (3) canary, eagle, pigeon, magpie   ....
    (4) lawyer, butcher, engineer, doctor   ....
    (5) beetle, ant, bee, locust   ....
    (6) omnibus, tramcar, lorry, wagon   ....
    (7) daffodil, tulip, violet, crocus   ....
    (8) cup, saucer, bowl, plate   ....
    (9) flounder, haddock, trout, herring   ....
   (10) autumn, winter, spring, summer   ....
   (11) shoes, Wellingtons, boots, slippers ....
   (12) potato, carrot, beetroot, turnip   ....
   (13) hawthorn, palm, beech, chestnut   ....
   (14) bread, butter, meat, porridge   ....
   (15) bramble, orange, banana, lemon   ....
   (16) water, milk, brine, paraffin   ....
   (17) wheat, maize, oats, barley   ....
   (18) aunt, uncle, niece, cousin   ....
   (19) twelve, seven, twenty, eight   ....
   (20) football, hockey, rugby, cricket   ....

2.   **In the following lists of words, one word seems out of place. Underline the word you consider is not in the same class.** No. 1 is done for you.

   (1) Rose, daffodil, tulip, <u>cauliflower</u>, carnation.

   (2) Hen, hare, duck, goose, turkey.

   (3) Beech, elm, oak, violet, ash.

   (4) Slate, gold, silver, iron, lead.

   (5) Potato, turnip, lemon, carrot, beetroot.

   (6) Granite, cement, limestone, marble, whinstone.

   (7) Oats, wheat, scone, barley, rye.

   (8) Salmon, whale, herring, mackerel, cod.

   (9) Diamond, emerald, pearl, ruby, sapphire.

 (10) Glasgow, London, Paris, Lisbon, Rome.

 (11) Ireland, Sri Lanka, Iceland, Malta, Spain.

 (12) Tea, coffee, biscuit, cocoa, Ovaltine.

 (13) Rain, sleet, snow, heat, hail.

 (14) Bacon, milk, cheese, butter, bread.

 (15) Shield, lance, dagger, gun, spear.

 (16) Omnibus, tractor, liner, train, tram.

 (17) Cottage, mansion, palace, bungalow, warehouse.

 (18) Tomatoes, journeys, excursions, voyages, trips.

 (19) Birch, maize, maple, chestnut, pine.

 (20) Man, boy, master, princess, uncle.

 (21) Rose, palm, orchid, lily, primrose.

 (22) John, Joseph, Jane, James, Jacob.

 (23) Cupboard, kitchen, scullery, bedroom, parlour.

 (24) Orange, potato, cherry, apple, banana.

 (25) Oil, milk, calico, wine, water.

 (26) Boy, wagon, kitten, girl, puppy.

 (27) Plate, cup, saucer, bowl, fork.

 (28) Radiator, violin, flute, piano, cornet.

 (29) France, Germany, London, Italy, Spain.

 (30) Elephant, tiger, giraffe, crocodile, horse.

 (31) Salt, sauce, plate, mustard, pepper.

 (32) Spinster, lady, niece, uncle, sister.

 (33) Chair, carpet, wardrobe, stool, table.

 (34) Baker, miner, tobacconist, draper, barber.

 (35) Pigeon, parrot, penguin, sparrow, swallow.

 (36) Basket, purse, kettle, trunk, scabbard.

Classification

3. **Put a line under one of the same kind as the first three in each line.**
No. 1 is done for you.

(1)	Cap, balmoral, hat	face, boot, <u>turban</u>, coat, hatchet.
(2)	Jug, tea-pot, cup	bowl, loaf, hammer, key, door.
(3)	Stork, hen, eagle	egg, butterfly, owl, nest, mouse.
(4)	Tulip, daisy, violet	foot, cup, brush, rose, scissors.
(5)	Eye, nose, mouth	hand, leg, knee, arm, ear.
(6)	Tin, copper, zinc	basin, iron, marble, corn, carrot.
(7)	Tuna, whiting, mackerel	gate, street, orange, ship, trout.
(8)	Chair, table, stool	sofa, pot, door, car, tub.
(9)	Buffalo, monkey, squirrel	wasp, herring, skunk, canary.
(10)	Apple, banana, plum	peach, violet, onion, hawthorn.
(11)	Iron, lead, copper	marble, coal, slate, zinc.
(12)	Ant, earwig, moth	rabbit, fly, poodle, snake.
(13)	Nairobi, London, Kingston	Trinidad, Scotland, Kenya, Lagos.
(14)	Steamer, yacht, submarine	aeroplane, trawler, motor, train.
(15)	Caramel, cake, ice-cream	book, pencil, toffee, ruler.
(16)	Falcon, penguin, raven	grasshopper, maple, stoat, heron.
(17)	Frock, jacket, coat	blouse, curtain, sheet, carpet.
(18)	Motor, train, taxi	bicycle, steamer, canoe, seaplane.
(19)	Salmon, flounder, haddock	vulture, snail, eel, setter.
(20)	Tennis, hockey, golf	darts, cricket, boxing, whist.
(21)	Crocus, tulip, hyacinth	chestnut, turnip, lily, ruby.
(22)	Cocoa, coffee, water	bread, soup, pepper, sugar.
(23)	Violin, piano, harp	drum, bugle, guitar, trombone.
(24)	Cabbage, carrot, potato	lilac, beetroot, pine, pheasant.
(25)	Barber, florist, draper	milliner, labourer, miner, pedlar.
(26)	Ankle, foot, knee	head, wrist, thigh, nose.
(27)	Scuttle, vase, caddy	jotter, shovel, window, bin.
(28)	Terrier, collie, greyhound	tiger, spaniel, hyena, lion.
(29)	Sandals, shoes, boots	gloves, trousers, slippers, pockets.
(30)	Oak, elm, beech	pansy, teak, daisy, lettuce.

Classification

Underline the word (in brackets) which has a **similar meaning** to the first three words in each line. No. 1 is done for you.

(1) Cost, fee, charge (money, <u>price</u>, purse, silver).

(2) Mount, soar, rise (depart, arrive, retire, ascend).

(3) Hail, greet, salute (alarm, habit, welcome, ignore).

(4) Vigilant, alert, wary (aloft, believe, attempt, watchful).

(5) Notice, perceive, behold (provide, observe, advise, obtain).

(6) Concluded, finished, ended (commenced, allowed, completed, carried).

(7) Peace, calm, rest (quietness, worry, agitated, movement).

(8) Support, help, aid (abandon, remedy, assist, ignore).

(9) Walked, tramped, marched (chuckled, plodded, glanced, knocked).

(10) Conquer, defeat, overcome (bully, retire, vanquish, submit).

(11) Edge, border, fringe (margin, centre, interior, cover).

(12) Occupied, diligent, busy (lazy, helpless, indolent, industrious).

(13) Hinder, retard, delay (progress, obstruct, reveal, select).

(14) Vagabond, wanderer, tramp (milliner, caddie, collector, vagrant).

(15) Desert, forsake, leave (protect, abandon, pursue, arrive).

(16) Serious, sober, solemn (blunt, grave, tired, insulted).

(17) Weep, cry, wail (deafen, bite, whimper, frighten).

(18) Pleased, happy, delighted (friendly, agreeable, kind, cheerful).

(19) Stupid, silly, foolish (stylish, trivial, absurd, helpless).

(20) Annoy, pester, torment (deceive, irritate, influence, hinder).

GRADATION

There are five words in each row. You are asked to place them in order of size (smallest first). No. 1 is done for you.

1. boy, baby, man, child, youth.
   baby, child, boy, youth, man.

2. ten, one, million, thousand, hundred.
   ....

3. litre, millilitre, decalitre, decilitre, hectolitre.
   ....

4. gallon, pint, bushel, quart, gill.
   ....

5. inch, furlong, foot, mile, yard.
   ....

6. minute, week, second, hour, day.
   ....

7. cow, cat, elephant, sheep, mouse.
   ....

8. kettle, cup, pail, teapot, tub.
   ....

9. mansion, hut, bungalow, cottage, palace.
   ....

10. metre, centimetre, kilometre, millimetre.
    ....

11. shark, sardine, whale, cod, haddock.
    ....

12. hen, pigeon, robin, ostrich, turkey.
    ....

13. city, country, town, continent, village.
    ....

14. bean, pea, cabbage, onion, turnip.
    ....

15. ocean, river, spring, stream, sea.
    ....

16. plum, currant, orange, cherry, melon.

   . . . .

17. piano, trombone, pipe-organ, violin, flute.

   . . . .

18. wallet, purse, safe, vault, handbag.

   . . . .

19. fly, midge, ant, wasp, butterfly.

   . . . .

20. sentence, letter, paragraph, word, chapter.

   . . . .

Here are some harder examples. Grade each group of five words according to the word in the bracket (least first):

(sound)   giggled, laughed, smiled, guffawed, chuckled.

   . . . .

(feeling) punched, touched, battered, tapped, knocked.

   . . . .

(speed)   strode, galloped, trotted, cantered, walked.

   . . . .

(sound)   shrieked, talked, shouted, whispered, roared.

   . . . .

(feeling) fingered, slapped, patted, caressed, walloped.

   . . . .

(speed)   marched, sauntered, strode, walked, shuffled.

   . . . .

(sound)   crooned, hummed, lilted, yodelled, sang.

   . . . .

(time)   looked, stared, glimpsed, gazed, glanced.

   . . . .

ASSOCIATION

Underline the two words in the brackets which are associated with (or part of) the first word in bold type. No. 1 is done for you.

1. **boot**   (sleeve, heel, handle, sole, paper).

2. **chair**   (saucer, poker, arm, tongs, leg).

3. **bed**   (mattress, carpet, ribbon, blanket, blouse).

4. **bath**   (book, soap, glove, vase, sponge).

5. **fireplace** (jacket, refrigerator, fender, oven, stocking).

6. **tree**   (wall, trunk, chalk, bough, lamp).

7. **clock**   (hands, wristlet, face, shovel, cushion).

8. **flower**   (purse, stem, seat, lard, petals).

9. **bird**   (sheet, wings, beak, canoe, factory).

10. **bee**   (sting, mirror, bread, honey, banana).

11. **knife**   (acorn, blade, opposite, handle, coat).

12. **kettle**   (spout, plate, butter, basket, lid).

13. **window**   (spoon, glass, pillow, bullet, curtains).

14. **motor**   (chart, anvil, engine, tyres, grate).

15. **sun**   (rays, harbour, sermon, heat, crescent).

16. **bottle**   (handle, paper, chimney, neck, cork).

17. **rifle**   (barrel, trigger, candle, mirror, arrow).

18. **fork**   (cellar, prongs, beggar, handle, blade).

19. **fish**   (fodder, arms, gills, mutton, fins).

20. **torch**   (bulb, furnace, battery, meter, grate).

21. **door**   (model, knob, disease, drawer, hinges).

22. **bicycle**   (pedals, hangar, bowl, pump, gangway).

23. **pillow**   (rug, slip, cloak, bolster, pinafore).

24. **ship**   (hood, melody, bridge, trolley, bow).

25. **aeroplane** (funnel, wings, tail, tunnel, paddle).

26. **horse**   (bridle, crystal, branch, mane, horns).

27. **fire**   (errand, smoke, boots, comb, flame).

28. **piano**   (buttons, fatigue, keys, pedals, pencil).

29. **potato**   (forest, peelings, bark, gown, chips).

30. **hat**   (crown, glue, pouch, brim, pocket).

31. **vehicle**   (velvet, brakes, wheels, cotton, scissors).

32. **window**   (cords, pane, basin, inventor, easel).

33. **boot**   (knuckle, hatchet, upper, jacket, tongue).

34. **pipe**   (granite, towel, packet, bowl, stem).

35. **tree**   (fork, telegraph, foliage, muslin, cabbage).

36. **fruit**   (marble, core, turnip, rind, salmon).

37. **motor-car** (parrot, article, radiator, exhaust, pilgrim).

38. **house**   (compartment, gable, cock-pit, scuppers, eaves).

39. **telephone** (paragraph, scabbard, receiver, needle, booth).

40. **barrel**   (fatigue, staves, square, hoops, spokes).

Here are more examples with particular reference to parts of our body and their actions:

    ear   (deafness, cantered, listening, noticed, tumbled).

    mouth (pushed, strode, glancing, tasting, chewing).

    nose   (smiled, sniffed, walked, odour, roared).

    eye   (sang, lashes, laughed, blinked, swinging).

    face   (folded, smile, yodelled, grin, toddled).

    head   (muttered, sauntered, ache, flying, nodding).

    arms   (trotted, mumbled, folded, waving, chanted).

    hands (writing, strolling, kicking, wink, clasp).

    legs   (crooned, crossed, fingered, smiling, running).

    feet   (dancing, waving, paddling, shouting, grinning).

ANALOGIES

Put in the suitable words in the spaces below:

Example: **Little** is to **big** as **dwarf** is to **giant**.

1. **Spider** is to **fly** as **cat** is to ....

2. **Sheep** is to **mutton** as **pig** is to ....

3. **Steamer** is to **pier** as **train** is to ....

4. **Boy** is to **girl** as .... is to **woman**.

5. **June** is to **July** as .... is to **May**.

6. **High** is to **low** as .... is to **down**.

7. **North** is to .... as **east** is to **west**.

8. **Uncle** is to .... as **aunt** is to **niece**.

9. **Soldier** is to .... as **sailor** is to **navy**.

10. .... is to **donkey** as **neigh** is to **horse**.

11. .... is to **hand** as **toe** is to **foot**.

12. .... are to **birds** as **scales** are to **fish**.

13. **Tear** is to **sorrow** as **smile** is to ....

14. **Wrist** is to **arm** as **ankle** is to ....

15. **One** is to **dozen** as **dozen** is to ....

16. **Arrow** is to **bow** as .... is to **rifle**.

17. **Cat** is to **kitten** as .... is to **pup**.

18. **Foot** is to **man** as .... is to **horse**.

19. **Father** is to .... as **mother** is to **daughter**.

20. **Artist** is to .... as **author** is to **book**.

21. **Water** is to .... as **liquid** is to **solid**.

22. .... is to **cygnet** as **pig** is to **porkling**.

23. .... is to **herring** as **school** is to **whales**.

24. .... is to **hive** as **cow** is to **byre**.

25. **Wing** is to **bird** as **fin** is to ....

26. **Rich** is to **poor** as **ancient** is to ....

27. **One** is to **single** as **two** is to ....

44

28. **Flock** is to **sheep** as .... is to **cattle**.
29. **Here** is to **there** as .... is to **that**.
30. **Day** is to **week** as .... is to **year**.
31. **Eat** is to .... as **go** is to **went**.
32. **Oil** is to .... as **tea** is to **caddy**.
33. **Steam** is to .... as **smoke** is to **fire**.
34. .... is to **sty** as **horse** is to **stable**.
35. .... is to **cold** as **seldom** is to **often**.
36. .... is to **fish** as **air** is to **bird**.
37. **Table** is to **wood** as **window** is to ....
38. **Food** is to **hungry** as **drink** is to ....
39. **Statue** is to **sculptor** as **book** is to ....
40. **Wheel** is to **spoke** as **flower** is to ....
41. **Nose** is to **smell** as .... is to **taste**.
42. **Wrist** is to **cuff** as .... is to **collar**.
43. **Walk** is to **legs** as .... is to **wings**.
44. **Island** is to **sea** as .... is to **land**.
45. **Knife** is to .... as **gun** is to **shoot**.
46. **Picture** is to .... as **carpet** is to **floor**.
47. **Graceful** is to .... as **polite** is to **rude**.
48. **Descend** is to .... as **ascend** is to **height**.
49. .... is to **pipes** as **electricity** is to **wires**.
50. .... is to **church** as **tower** is to **castle**.
51. .... is to **forest** as **sheep** is to **flock**.
52. .... is to **egg** as **rind** is to **orange**.
53. **Constable** is to **thief** as **gamekeeper** is to ....
54. **Whisper** is to **shout** as **walk** is to ....
55. **Battery** is to **torch** as **bolster** is to ....
56. **Hearing** is to **ear** as **sight** is to ....

IT MAKES YOU THINK

1. Here is a list of Christmas presents which arrived at the Browns' house:

    diary, razor, knitting-bag, chocolates, saw, cigarettes, grapes and a fishing-rod.

    (a) **Mr. Brown** has a beard, likes woodwork, but does not smoke.

    (b) **Mrs. Brown** is ill in bed, but able to sit up and use her hands.

    (c) **John Brown** is twenty years old, clean-shaven, and does not like fishing.

    (d) **Mary Brown** is twelve years old, keen on writing, and fond of sweets.

    Distribute the presents on the above list to each member of the family.

2. On one side of my street the homes all have odd numbers, ending with the baker's which is No. 17. On the other side the numbers are all even, ending with the draper's which is No. 18. Fred Thomson is my next-door-neighbour and his house is No. 10. You pass my house when walking from the draper's to Fred's house. **What number is my house?**

3. A policeman was on his rounds one night when he saw a man with a box under his arm come out of a house and hurry down the street. Later the constable found that some jewels had been stolen from the house. The officer remembered that the man he had seen wore a long black coat. He had also noticed that the man had a beard and was lame in his right leg. Next day the following four men were detained:

    John Smith — bearded, long black coat, lame in left leg.

    Tom Taylor — bearded, short black coat, lame in right leg.

    Jack Jones — lame in right leg, short black coat, bearded.

    Jim Baker — long black coat, lame in right leg, bearded.

    If you were the policeman, whom would you consider guilty?

4. The sentences below, when properly arranged, form a short story. Indicate their correct order by numbering them from **1** to **5** within the brackets:

( ) The lad was cast ashore on a lonely island near the scene of the tragedy.

( ) After many exciting adventures he returned to England, none the worse for his experience.

( ) Robinson Crusoe went to sea when he was nineteen years of age.

( ) Luckily he managed to obtain from the wreck, many things which proved useful to him during his stay on the island.

( ) On his first voyage, the ship encountered a terrible storm and foundered on a rock.

5. In a very dark cupboard there is a heap of twenty socks, all of the same size, ten of which are grey and ten blue. **How many socks must you pick up** in order to make sure that you obtain **a pair of the same colour?**

6. My clock has gone wrong and chimes three times at one o'clock, four times at two o'clock, and so on. It is also half-an-hour fast. **What is the correct time when the clock has just chimed eight?**

7. Tom is twice as old as Mary, but he is two years younger than Jim. **What is Mary's age** if Jim will be twenty years old in two years' time?

AN ODD WORD OR TWO

Where does a man buy a cap for his knee,
Or a key for a lock of his hair?
Should his eyes be called an academy
Because there are pupils there?

In the crown of his head what gems are found?
Who crosses the bridge of his nose?
Can he use, if a picture requires to be hung,
The nails on the ends of his toes?

If the crook of his elbow is put in gaol,
I'd say, "What did he do?"
But how does he sharpen his shoulder-blades?
I'm hanged if I know. Do you?

ABSURDITIES

Anything which is absurd is utterly foolish and unreasonable. Can you explain what is absurd in the following?

1. I had six pencils altogether and gave away three of them to my little brother. I had nine pencils left.

2. To sweeten his tea the boy put a spoonful of salt in it.

3. The man is not so tall as he was when a baby.

4. The express train sped along swiftly and silently as it had square wheels.

5. I hope to attend the concert which took place last week.

6. The witness was asked, "Were you near the horse when it kicked you?"

7. A tramp, wishing to lengthen his blanket, took a bit off the top and added it to the bottom.

8. "Kind sir! Please give me a copper as I am deaf and dumb," cried the old beggar.

9. "Keep moving, please! If everybody was to stand there, how would the rest of the people manage to get past?"

10. The storm, which began yesterday, has continued for three days without a break.

11.   "The elephant is a bonnie bird,
             It flits from bough to bough,
             It makes its nest in the rhubarb tree,
             And whistles like a cow."

12.   "'Twas in the month of Liverpool,
             In the city of July,
             The rain was snowing heavily,
             And the streets were very dry."

13. Two Eskimos were having a chat. The weather was so cold that, when one of them spoke, his words froze into blocks of ice. The other had to melt the blocks on a frying pan in order to find out what his friend had been saying to him.

14. One day at the seaside a man dived from a high platform. When he was half-way down he suddenly noticed that the tide was out and that he would strike his head on the rocks below. This frightened him so much that he changed his mind and jumped back to the platform.

15. A father wrote to his son, "I enclose a postal order. If you do not receive this letter, please let me know at once."

16. A magician was showing his favourite trick. From the roof of the stage hung a long rope, at the end of which was a hook. An assistant entered and placed a pail of water on the hook. Waving his hands and shouting some strange words, the conjurer covered the pail of water with a magic cloth. A few seconds later he snatched the cloth away and, lo and behold! — the pail had disappeared and the water was left hanging on the hook.

17. It is much safer to travel in a motor-car than in a train, because in a train accident hundreds of people may be injured, while in a motor-car accident there are never more than a few people injured.

18. The proud owner said to his friend, "This clock is so old that the moving shadow of the pendulum has worn away the wood at the back."

19. In some countries it is against the law for a man to marry his widow's sister.

20. Old John Smith lived in a small cottage, which stood on the top of a barren hill and faced the east. From the foot of the hill a grassy plain stretched in every direction as far as the eye could see. On the evening of John's thirtieth birthday, while he was sitting on the front door-step, watching the setting sun, he noticed a horseman riding down to the cottage. The trees made it difficult for him to see clearly, but he perceived that the horseman had only one arm. When, however, he got a closer view, he recognised the visitor as his son James, who had left home some twenty years before. On seeing his father, James immediately dismounted, ran towards him, and threw his arms round his neck.

ABBREVIATIONS

An abbreviation is the shortening of a word to fewer letters. These letters are used in place of a word for brevity. It used to be customary to mark all abbreviations with a full stop. Now it is quite correct either to use stops or to omit them. In some cases using the stop helps to avoid confusion, e.g. A.1.

Abbreviation	Word in Full	Meaning
A.A.	Automobile Association	
A.B.	Able-bodied seaman	
A.D.	*Anno Domini*	in the year of our Lord
a.m.	*ante meridiem*	before noon
A.1		First class (of ships)
B.A.	Bachelor of Arts	
B.B.	Boys' Brigade	
BBC	British Broadcasting Corporation	
B.C.	Before Christ	
B.D.	Bachelor of Divinity	
B.L.	Bachelor of Law	
B.M.A.	British Medical Association	
B.R.	British Rail	
B.Sc.	Bachelor of Science	
C.	Centigrade or Celsius	
C.A.	Chartered Accountant	
Ch.B.	Bachelor of Surgery	
C.I.D.	Criminal Investigation Department	
Co.	Company or County	
C.O.D.	Cash on Delivery	
Cr.	Credit	
curt.	current	this month
do.	ditto	the same
Dr.	Doctor	
D.V.	*Deo volente*	God willing
EEC or EC	European (Economic) Community	
e.g.	*exempli gratia*	for example
E.R.	Elizabeth Regina	Queen Elizabeth
Esq.	Esquire	
etc.	*et cetera*	and the rest
F.	Fahrenheit	
GCE	General Certificate of Education	
GCSE	General Certificate of Secondary Education	

Abbreviation	Word in Full	Meaning
G.P.O.	General Post Office	
H.E.	His (or Her) Excellency	
H.M.	Her Majesty	
H.M.S.	Her Majesty's Ship	
h.p.	horse-power	
H.R.H.	His (or Her) Royal Highness	
i.e. or ie	*id est*	that is
Inst.	Instant	this month
IMF	International Monetary Fund	
I.O.U.	I owe you	
J.P.	Justice of the Peace	
Lat.	Latitude	
LL.B.	Bachelor of Laws	
lbw	leg before wicket	
Ltd.	Limited	
M.A.	Master of Arts	
Messrs.	messieurs	gentlemen
M.P.	Member of Parliament	
Mr.	Mister	
Mrs.	Mistress	
Ms.	Miss or Mistress	
MSS.	Manuscripts	
N.A.T.O.	North Atlantic Treaty Organisation	
N.B.	*nota bene*	note well
No.	Numero	Number
O.H.M.S.	On Her Majesty's Service	
O.K.		all correct
PAYE	Pay as You Earn	
p.c.	post card	
per cent	*per centum*	in each hundred
P.C.	Police constable, Privy Councillor	
p.m.	*post meridiem*	after noon
P.O.	Post Office or Postal Order	
Pres.	President	
prox.	*proximo*	next month
P.S.	*post scriptum*	written after
P.T.O	Please turn over	
R.A.C.	Royal Automobile Club	
R.A.F.	Royal Air Force	

Abbreviations

Abbreviation	Word in Full	Meaning
R.C.	Roman Catholic	
R.I.P.	*Requiescat in pace*	May he (or she) rest in peace
R.N.	Royal Navy	
R.N.R.	Royal Naval Reserve	
R.S.V.P.	*Repondez s'il vous plait*	Reply if you please
S.A.	Salvation Army	
SCE	Scottish Certificate of Education	
S.S.	Steam-ship or Sailing-ship	
T.A.	Territorial Army	
T.U.C.	Trades Union Congress	
U.K.	United Kingdom	
ult.	*ultimo*	last month
U.N.O.	United Nations Organisation	
U.N.E.S.C.O.	United Nations Educational, Scientific and Cultural Organisation	
U.S.A.	United States of America	
v	versus	against
viz.	*videlicet*	namely
W.P.	weather permitting	
Y.M.C.A.	Young Men's Christian Association	
Y.W.C.A.	Young Women's Christian Association	

CONTRACTIONS

auto	automobile	photo	photograph
bus	omnibus	piano	pianoforte
cello	violoncello	plane	aeroplane
exam	examination	pram	perambulator
gym	gymnasium	prom	promenade
mag	magazine	specs	spectacles
phone	telephone		

Exercises on Abbreviations

1. *(a)* What do the following abbreviations mean?
   J.P., BBC, C.O.D., M.P., G.P.O., B.C., M.A., H.R.H., lbw,
   B.R.

   (b) Often abbreviations are used in letter-writing. Give the meaning
   of the following:
   a.m., inst., prox., ult., Esq., Mr., W.P., p.m., St.

2. Give customary abbreviations for:

   (a) Monday, Tuesday, Wednesday, Friday, Saturday, January,
   February, August, September, October, November, December.

   (b) Ounces, pounds (weight), hundredweights, pints, gallons,
   seconds, minutes, hours, inches, feet, yards, miles.

   (c) Millimetres, centimetres, metres, kilometres, millilitres,
   centilitres, litres, milligrams, grammes, kilograms, millions.

3. Write the following with all abbreviated terms in full:

   (a) Robt. Brown, Esq.,
       74 Abbey Rd.,
       Glasgow.

   (b) Dr. Thos. Smith, M.P., a brother of the famous Harley St.
   surgeon who recently toured the U.S.A., was married on the 4th
   inst. in St. Margaret's Chapel, Westminster.

4. Write the following sentences, using the customary abbreviations:

   (a) William Miller, able-bodied seaman of Her Majesty's Ship
   Newcastle, was awarded the Victoria Cross for gallantry in action.

   (b) Mister George Woods, a well-known local Justice of the Peace,
   was appointed managing director of Messieurs Cook and
   Company, Limited.

5. Where contractions have been used in the following sentences, give the
   words in full:

   (a) We boarded a train as the bus was full.

   (b) The specs were discovered in the pram.

   (c) I saw his photo in a weekly mag.

   (d) He phoned for news of the missing plane.

   (e) The exam was held in the gym.

ANTONYMS

WORDS OPPOSITE IN MEANING

Give the words opposite in meaning to the following:

abroad	depth	go	never	small
absence	die	good	new	smart
accept	difficult	guilty	night	smooth
adult	dirty	hard	noise	sober
alive	disperse	hate	none	soft
ancestor	divide	heavy	north	solid
ancient	down	height	nowhere	south
answer	drunk	hell	numerous	sour
arrive	dry	here	often	spacious
asleep	dull	hero	old	spendthrift
assemble	dwarf	heroic	opaque	stale
back	early	hide	open	stationary
backward	east	high	out	steep
bad	easy	hollow	past	stern
barren	ebb	home	peace	straight
beautiful	educated	honest	pedestrian	strong
bent	empty	hot	permanent	stupid
better	enemy	humble	plain	success
big	entrance	ignorant	pleasant	summer
bitter	evening	immense	plural	superior
black	ever	inferior	polite	sweet
bless	everywhere	innocent	poor	take
bold	exit	join	poverty	tall
bottom	expand	junior	powerful	tame
bow	failure	juvenile	praise	temporary
bright	faint	land	present	there
broad	fair	last	private	these
buy	fair-play	late	prosperity	those
captive	false	lean	proud	timid
captivity	familiar	liberty	purchase	tiny
cheap	famous	light	question	top
chubby	fancy	live	quiet	transparent
clean	far	long	rapid	truth
clever	fat	lost	refuse	ugly
coarse	feeble	loud	retire	unite
cold	fertile	love	retreat	vacant
come	few	low	reveal	vague
conceal	first	mad	rich	valley

54

condemn	flow	maximum	right	victory
confined	foe	merry	rude	wane
confirm	foolish	minimum	sadness	war
contract	foreign	minority	safety	wax
correct	found	miser	seldom	weak
coward	free	miserable	selfish	wealth
curse	freedom	modern	sell	west
damp	friend	morning	senior	wet
dark	front	motorist	shallow	white
day	frown	mountain	short	wild
deep	full	moving	show	wise
defeat	future	multiply	shut	worse
defend	gaunt	narrow	singular	wrong
deny	generous	native	slovenly	young
depart	giant	near	slow	youth

Give the words opposite in meaning to the following:

By Adding Prefix

advantage	direct	legible	order	safe
approve	essential	like	patient	sane
audible	fair	lock	perfect	screw
aware	famous	loyal	pleasure	selfish
behave	fire	modest	poisonous	sense
comfortable	happy	moral	polite	tidy
common	human	mortal	possible	transitive
connect	just	necessary	proper	trust
content	kind	noble	pure	twist
convenient	known	normal	regular	visible
correct	legal	obey	reverent	wise

By Changing the Prefix

Ascend, encourage, export, exterior, external, increase, inside.

By Changing the Suffix

Careful, cheerful, joyful, merciful, pitiful, useful.

55

Antonyms

The following may be said to be Opposites:

author	reader	judge	prisoner
detective	thief	king	subject
doctor	patient	lawyer	client
driver	conductor	leader	follower
employer	employee	parent	child
gamekeeper	poacher	policeman	criminal
guardian	ward	shopkeeper	customer
host	guest	speaker	listener
hound	quarry	teacher	pupil

EXERCISES

1. Write words opposite in meaning to:

   success, visible, praise, transparent, fair-play, arrive, nowhere, barren, ancient, wise.

2. Give the opposites (by prefix) of the following:

   audible, behave, known, legible, modest, noble, obedient, regular, sense, pleasant.

3. In the spaces provided write the opposites of each of the following:

north	....	possible	....
entrance	....	often	....
rough	....	enemy	....
pedestrian	....	bitter	....
guilty	....	senior	....

4. Give the opposites of the adjectives in the following phrases:

a bright boy	a bright colour	a bright light
a stormy day	a stormy sea	a stormy meeting
a wild boy	a wild horse	a wild flower

5. State the opposites of:

an armed man	a false gift	a soft answer
I am sorry	a heavy load	a mighty army
to keep step	to sing in tune	she was dark

56

6. In the spaces provided write the opposites of the words underlined:

   Example: The ball was solid — hollow

   (1) It was a beautiful dress ....
   (2) Tuesday was a very sunny day ....
   (3) The ascent of the hill took two hours ....
   (4) He has a temporary post ....
   (5) She purchased the toy ....
   (6) He is a lazy fellow ....
   (7) There was an abundance of fruit ....
   (8) He gave an intelligent answer ....
   (9) The sea was rough. ....
   (10) It was very fertile land ....

7. Fill in the blanks in the following sentences with a word which is the opposite of the word underlined:

   (1) Read the question and then write your ....
   (2) The Polar bear which escaped from the zoo was soon ....
   (3) Last year the well was empty but this year it is ....
   (4) A polite boy is much thought of: there is nothing to be gained by being ....
   (5) I suddenly remembered that I had .... my spectacles.

8. Re-write the following sentences, putting in words opposite in meaning to those underlined:

   (1) In the morning the sun rises in the east.
   (2) The hero was praised for his fair-play.
   (3) The fancy box was big and heavy.
   (4) Profits on superior articles made him rich.
   (5) The mighty army advanced after its success.

SYNONYMS

WORDS SIMILAR IN MEANING

abandon	leave	enormous	gigantic
abode	dwelling	extended	enlarged
abundant	plentiful	exterior	outside
accused	blamed	fall	drop
acute	sharp	famous	noted
adhere	stick	fatigue	weariness
affectionate	loving	feeble	weak
aid	help	gap	hole
ally	friend	glance	look
amazement	wonder	gravely	sternly
ancient	old	greeted	saluted
assemble	gather	grope	feel
astonish	surprise	gruff	harsh
asunder	apart	halt	stop
blank	empty	heroic	brave
bright	shining	hoax	trick
broad	wide	imitate	copy
caution	care	insolent	rude
circular	round	intention	purpose
coarse	rough	interior	inside
commence	begin	join	unite
comprehend	understand	lament	grieve
conceal	hide	lean	thin
constable	policeman	lofty	high
conversation	talk	loyal	true
courage	bravery	mad	insane
cunning	sly	malady	disease
curb	control	margin	edge
custom	habit	mariner	sailor
deceive	cheat	marsh	swamp
difficult	hard	maximum	most
disaster	calamity	meagre	scanty
dusk	twilight	minimum	least
elude	escape	moan	groan
emperor	king	modern	new
enemy	foe	moisture	dampness

58

mute	dumb	robust	strong
myth	fable	scene	sight
nimble	agile	shrine	tomb
noisy	rowdy	sleek	smooth
odour	smell	slender	slim
omen	sign	small	little
option	choice	squirming	wriggling
peculiar	strange	steed	horse
persuade	coax	stern	strict
plume	feather	stubborn	obstinate
profit	gain	sturdy	strong
prohibit	forbid	surrender	yield
prompt	quick	suspended	hung
powerful	strong	terror	fear
protect	guard	tested	tried
puny	weak	thrust	pushed
purchase	buy	tranquil	peaceful
quaint	odd	transparent	clear
quantity	amount	unite	join
queer	peculiar	vacant	empty
raiment	clothes	valour	bravery
ramble	roam	vanquish	defeat
rank	position	wealth	riches
rapid	quick	wicked	sinful
regret	sorrow	withdraw	retire
remedy	cure	wrath	anger
residence	dwelling	wretched	miserable
reveal	show	yearly	annually
roam	wander		

EXERCISES

1. Give words similar in meaning to the following:

comprehend, empty, sufficient, vicinity, attempted, enemies, risky, purchase, perceive, modern.

Synonyms

2. In the spaces provided write words similar in meaning:

bright	....	peculiar	....
convenient	....	lofty	....
disappear	....	unite	....
hoax	....	margin	....
valour	....	wrath	....

3. Place the words in their proper positions in the sentence:

(handsome — pretty)   The .... girl admired the .... prince.

(proud — vain)   The .... king laughed at the .... little girl.

(fat — stout)   A .... woman should not eat .... meat.

(feeble — weak)   .... tea will not refresh the .... old lady.

(hot — sultry)   On a .... day don't drink .... liquids.

(old — antique)   The .... man was fond of .... furniture.

(loving — tender)   Her .... hands had prepared a .... chicken.

(sad — dull)   The day was .... and we felt quite ....

4. Give short sentences, one for each word, showing the correct use of the following:

learn, teach, mad, angry, invent, discover, possible, probable, accept, except.

5. Use similar words in place of the words underlined:

(1) The pail <u>dropped</u> into the well.

(2) "Don't <u>conceal</u> your real feelings."

(3) I was <u>astonished</u> to find the house <u>vacant</u>.

(4) He <u>alters</u> his plans <u>annually</u>.

HOMONYMS AND HOMOPHONES

A Homonym is a word having the same sound, and perhaps the same spelling, as another, but with a different meaning. Where the spelling of the words is different the words may also be known as Homophones (sounding the same). The following homonyms are all of the homophone variety.

air	heir	feat	feet
aisle	isle, I'll	flew	flue
allowed	aloud	flour	flower
ant	aunt	foul	fowl
ate	eight	gait	gate
bad	bade	gamble	gambol
bail	bale	gilt	guilt
ball	bawl	grate	great
bare	bear	groan	grown
beach	beech	hail	hale
bell	belle	hair	hare
blew	blue	hear	here
boar	bore	heard	herd
board	bored	higher	hire
bough	bow	him	hymn
boy	buoy	hoard	horde
buy	by, bye	hole	whole
ceiling	sealing	holy	wholly
cellar	seller	hour	our
cereal	serial	key	quay
cheap	cheep	knew	new
check	cheque	knight	night
coarse	course	knot	not
collar	caller	knows	nose
core	corps	lair	layer
council	counsel	leak	leek
crews	cruise	lightening	lightning
currant	current	loan	lone
dear	deer	loot	lute
desert	dessert	made	maid
die	dye	mail	male
draft	draught	main	mane
ewe	you, yew	mare	mayor
faint	feint	meat	meet
fair	fare	medal	meddle

Homonyms and Homophones

missed	mist	sail	sale
more	mower	scene	seen
muscle	mussel	scent	sent, cent
none	nun	sea	see
oar	o'er, ore	seam	seem
pail	pale	sew	so, sow
pain	pane	sight	site
pair	pare, pear	soar	sore
pause	paws	sole	soul
peace	piece	son	sun
peal	peel	stair	stare
pearl	peril	stake	steak
peer	pier	stationary	stationery
piece	peace	steal	steel
place	plaice	stile	style
plain	plane	tail	tale
plum	plumb	tares	tears
pores	pours	tears	tiers
practice	practise	their	there
praise	prays, preys	threw	through
principal	principle	throne	thrown
profit	prophet	tide	tied
rains	reigns, reins	time	thyme
raise	rays, raze	to	too, two
read	reed	told	tolled
real	reel	vain	vane, vein
right	rite, wright, write	vale	veil
ring	wring	waist	waste
road	rode, rowed	wait	weight
root	route	weak	week
rose	rows	won	one
rye	wry	wood	would

EXERCISES

1. Make short sentences, one for each word, showing the correct use of
    the following:

    bear, bare, fool, full, flower, flour, too, two, ate, eight, write,
    right.

Homonyms and Homophones

2. Score out the wrong words:

> She bought some (steak, stake).
> The bicycle was for (sail, sale).
> We must (hire, higher) a motor-car.
> The (hole, whole) army marched into the town.
> The boy broke a (pane, pain) of glass.
> We walked to the golf (coarse, course).
> (Their, There) books are on the desks.
> The girl had to (wait, weight) till four o'clock.
> The wounded soldier uttered a loud (grown, groan).
> The joiner (bored, board) a small (whole, hole) in the (wood, would).

3. Give sentences, one for each word, showing clearly the meaning of each of the following words:

> collar, caller, steal, steel, heard, herd, reign, rain, their, there.

4. Insert the words in their proper places:

> (allowed — aloud)   It is not .... to speak .... in class.
>
> (maid — made)   The .... admitted that she had .... a mistake.
>
> (piece — peace)   He will give no .... until he receives a .... of cake.
>
> (scent — sent)   "Did you get the .... I .... you?"
>
> (stair — stare)   I saw him .... at the man on the ....
>
> (waist — waste)   ".............. not, want not," said the woman with the thin ....

5. Medal, horde, gambol, guilt, prophet, gamble, meddle, profit, gilt, hoard.

From the above list insert the correct words in the following sentences:

> A .... of coins was found under the floor.
> The business man made a large .... on the deal.
> He was told not to .... with the toys.
> I saw the lambs .... in the field.
> His name was printed in large .... letters.

Homonyms and Homophones

6. The answers are words that are pronounced alike but differ in meaning,
   e.g.

$$\left\{ \begin{array}{l} \text{no} \\ \text{cry of a horse} \end{array} \right. \qquad \begin{array}{l} \textbf{nay} \\ \textbf{neigh} \end{array}$$

(1) $\left\{ \begin{array}{l} \text{a female sheep} \\ \text{an evergreen tree} \end{array} \right.$ ....

(2) $\left\{ \begin{array}{l} \text{sandy shore} \\ \text{kind of tree} \end{array} \right.$ ....

(3) $\left\{ \begin{array}{l} \text{guided} \\ \text{a metal} \end{array} \right.$ ....

(4) $\left\{ \begin{array}{l} \text{opens lock} \\ \text{harbour} \end{array} \right.$ ....

(5) $\left\{ \begin{array}{l} \text{flat land} \\ \text{joiner's tool} \end{array} \right.$ ....

(6) $\left\{ \begin{array}{l} \text{suffering} \\ \text{piece of glass} \end{array} \right.$ ....

(7) $\left\{ \begin{array}{l} \text{something round} \\ \text{shout loudly} \end{array} \right.$ ....

(8) $\left\{ \begin{array}{l} \text{rough} \\ \text{place for golf} \end{array} \right.$ ....

(9) $\left\{ \begin{array}{l} \text{front of ship} \\ \text{branch of tree} \end{array} \right.$ ....

(10) $\left\{ \begin{array}{l} \text{gain} \\ \text{foretells future} \end{array} \right.$ ....

(11) $\left\{ \begin{array}{l} \text{a flight of steps} \\ \text{to look fixedly} \end{array} \right.$ ....

(12) $\left\{ \begin{array}{l} \text{sixty minutes} \\ \text{belonging to us} \end{array} \right.$ ....

(13) $\left\{ \begin{array}{l} \text{quietness} \\ \text{a part of anything} \end{array} \right.$ ....

(14) $\left\{ \begin{array}{l} \text{a stupid person} \\ \text{no empty space} \end{array} \right.$ ....

(15) $\left\{ \begin{array}{l} \text{in that place} \\ \text{belonging to them} \end{array} \right.$ ....

CORRECT USAGE

THE VERB

Verbs are **"doing"** words we say, giving **"doing"** a very broad meaning. Words for **being done**, even **existing** (doing nothing) are verbs. Sometimes a verb consists of **one** word, sometimes of **two** or **more**, e.g.

(a)	Dogs *bark*.	*(g)*	No words *were spoken*.
(b)	Tom *laughed*.	*(h)*	Guests *will be invited*.
(c)	*Is* Mary there?	*(i)*	The tiger *should have waited*.
(d)	*Go* away!	*(j)*	My house *was being repaired*.
(e)	The day *will come*.	*(k)*	You *must have been joking*.
(f)	The jet *is landing*.		

Note. One of the words in the verb is the **main** verb: the others are **auxiliaries** (helpers).

Underline the verbs in the following sentences:

1. Rain fell yesterday.
2. Day is dawning.
3. It is sunny today.
4. We have been robbed.
5. I do not smoke.
6. I could hardly see.
7. Uncle may be coming today.
8. We should have been patient.
9. You should not have been told.
10. They are not looking well.
11. The sheep were worried by dogs.
12. I was worried till you came.

Forms and Parts of Verbs. Different forms have different uses, e.g. for

singular and plural subjects	A dog *barks*; dogs *bark*
different pronoun subjects	I *think*; he *thinks*
present, past, future tense (time)	I *walk*; I *walked*; I *shall walk*
continuous, completed action	We *are looking*; we *have looked*.

The **Infinitive** (e.g. *to bark*, *to look*) is the basic form from which most other parts of most verbs can be formed.

The **Present** and **Past Participles** are partly verb and partly adjective.

The **Present Participle** is formed by adding *–ing* to the infinitive and is used with parts of the verb *to be* to form continuous tenses, as in *We are looking* (look + *ing*).

The **Past Participle** is usually formed by adding *–ed* to the infinitive and is used with parts of the verb *to have* to form perfect (completed action) tenses, as in *We have looked* (look + *ed*). **Irregular** verbs form their past participle in other ways. Examples are listed below. Some participles also serve purely as adjectives, e.g. A *dazzling* light; your story was *amusing*; my heart is *broken*; *cracked* cups.

65

The Verb

Tenses. Except in the case of the verb *to be*, the **Present Tense** has the same form as the infinitive (unless the subject is *he*, *she*, *it* or a noun, when *–s* or *–es* is added). To form the **Future Tense** we place *shall* or *will* in front of the infinitive. To form the **Past Tense** of **regular** verbs we add *–ed* to the infinitive. So we have:

Infinitive	Present Tense	Future Tense	Past Tense
(to) look	(I, they) look	(I, we) shall look	(I, etc.) looked
	(he, it) looks	(you, etc.) will look	

Thus in **regular** verbs the same form serves both the **Past Tense**, (I) *looked*, and the **Past Participle** (I have) *looked*.

Many **irregular** verbs, however, form them differently. Here are a few of them:

Present Tense	Past Tense	Past Participle	Present Tense	Past Tense	Past Participle
am	was	been	choose	chose	chosen
arise	arose	arisen	come	came	come
drive	drove	driven	do	did	done
awake	awoke	awakened	drink	drank	drunk
bear	bore	borne	eat	ate	eaten
beat	beat	beaten	fall	fell	fallen
begin	began	begun	fly	flew	flown
ring	rang	rung	forget	forgot	forgotten
sing	sang	sung	freeze	froze	frozen
swim	swam	swum	give	gave	given
bite	bit	bitten	go	went	gone
hide	hid	hidden	lie	lay	lain
blow	blew	blown	ride	rode	ridden
grow	grew	grown	write	wrote	written
know	knew	known	run	ran	run
draw	drew	drawn	shake	shook	shaken
break	broke	broken	tear	tore	torn
speak	spoke	spoken			

Errors. One of the worst errors in speech (and writing) is the use of the Past Participle instead of the Past Tense (e.g. I *seen* you; they *done* that), and the Past Tense instead of the Past Participle (e.g. Have you *broke* it; they have *went*). To tune your ear to the correct usage give each of the above Past Tenses a subject (e.g. *Tom drove*) and say it aloud; then put a subject with *have*, *has* or *had* in front of the Past Participle (e.g. *I had* driven) and say it aloud.

EXERCISES

1. Give the past tense of:

arise, break, cut, fall, keep, say, shake, drink, bite, choose.

2. Give the past participle of:

bear, drive, fly, give, hurt, ride, sell, speak, come, swim.

3. Give the present tense of:

ate, beaten, froze, hidden, blew, spoken, awoke, sold, lost.

4. *(a)* Give the present participle of:

throw, give, spring, fire, begin.

(b) Give the present infinitive of:

burn, speak, stand, sweep, drive.

5. Give the past tense and past participle of:

am, do, forget, grow, write, sing, tear, hide, go, begin.

6. Complete the following table:

Present Tense	Past Tense	Past Participle
I rise	I rose	I have risen
I forget	I	I have ....
I cut	....	....
I sing	....	....
I blow	....	....

7. Fill in each space correctly with one of these words:

rise, rose, raise, risen, raised.

(a) When he met the lady he .... his hat.

(b) Yesterday the boy .... at five o'clock.

(c) I saw him .... from his seat.

(d) She tried to .... the lid.

(e) The sun had .... in the sky.

8. Use the correct part of the verbs in the blank spaces:

(go) She had .... for a walk.

(see) He .... his uncle yesterday.

(fall) The old man .... asleep in his chair.

(awake) He was .... by the noise.

(dream) The boy was .... about pirates.

The Verb

In each of the sentences below there are groups of two words within brackets. One of the two words is correct, the other wrong. Underline the correct word.

1. We (drank, drunk) our tea before we (sung, sang) the carol.

2. After he had (ran, run) about 5 kilometres, he (sank, sunk) to the ground.

3. Some cloth is (wove, woven) from wool which has (grown, grew) on sheep.

4. He had (gave, given) me the parcel before he was (took, taken) a prisoner.

5. The timid creature was (drove, driven) into a narrow valley where it was soon (slew, slain) by the cruel tiger.

6. The vessel (sank, sunk) before they had (swam, swum) a great distance.

7. The tree had (fell, fallen) across the road and many of its branches were (broke, broken).

8. By the time the sun had (rose, risen) the aeroplane had (flown, flew) across the sea.

9. No sooner had he (spoke, spoken) than a deer (sprang, sprung) into our path.

10. He (began, begun) to look for the toy which he had (gave, given) to his brother.

11. The man had (threw, thrown) away the purse which was (stole, stolen) from the lady.

12. The jacket had been well (wore, worn) and the cloth had (shrank, shrunk).

13. After we had (ate, eaten) our supper we went to the pond which was (froze, frozen) over.

14. The picture was (drawn, drew) by a famous and wealthy artist who had (rose, risen) from poverty.

15. They had just (went, gone) when we were (saw, seen) by our friends.

16. A nest had (fell, fallen) to the ground, where it had been (blew, blown) by the wind.

17. The bell (rang, rung) just after I had (wrote, written) the letter.

THE ADJECTIVE

An **Adjective** is a word which qualifies or adds to the meaning of a noun.

(An old form for **Adjective** was **Ad-noun**.)

Adjectives may be divided into three main classes.

1. **Descriptive Adjectives.**

    Good, bad, hard, soft, old, young, pale, red.

    Example: The **old** man caught a **bad** cold.

2. **Adjective of Quantity.**

    (a) **Definite** (including numerals).

    One, seven, twenty, second, fifth, both, double.

    Example: Both players scored **three** goals in the **second** game.

    (b) **Indefinite.**

    All, any, few, many, much, several, some.

    Example: We met **several** boys who had caught **some** fish.

3. **Adjectives of Distinction.**

    (a) **Demonstrative.**

    This, that, these, those, yon, yonder.

    Example: This stone was found on **yonder** hill.

    (b) **Interrogative.**

    Which, what, whose.

    Example: Which book do you want?

    (c) **Distributive.**

    Each, every, either, neither.

    Example: He could go home by **either** route.

EXERCISES

Underline the **Adjectives** in the following sentences:

1. The tall gentleman wore a blue overcoat.
2. Little Jim was a delicate boy with pale cheeks.
3. The weather was wet and foggy.
4. The ugly old witch spoke in a hoarse cracked voice.
5. The lost ball was found near the garden gate.

Comparison of Adjectives

Adjectives can have three *degrees*: **Positive, Comparative, Superlative.**

The **Positive** is simply descriptive, describing a noun or pronoun, e.g. a *short* holiday; *beautiful* hats; *clever* pupils; this is *broken*.

The **Comparative** is used in comparing some creature, thing or group with **one** other (creature, thing or group), e.g. the *taller* of the two; *taller* than the rest; mice are *smaller* than rats. If the positive is a short word the comparative is usually formed by adding *–er* to the positive, e.g. fast–er; great–er.

The **Superlative** is used in comparing some creature, thing or group with **more than one** other, e.g. the *tallest* of the three; the *wisest* of men. It is usually formed by adding *–est* to the positive, if a short word. When one thing or creature is compared with more than one other **treated as a group**, the comparative is used, e.g. Tom is *taller* than *the rest of the class*.

Adjectives of three syllables or more and most adjectives of two syllables form their comparative by placing *more* in front of the positive, and the superlative by placing *most* in front.

Some adjectives have quite different words for the comparative and superlative.

Positive	Comparative	Superlative	Positive	Comparative	Superlative
(a)		Small word in positive			
big	bigger	biggest	late	later	latest
fast	faster	fastest	long	longer	longest
gay	gayer	gayest	small	smaller	smallest
great	greater	greatest	tall	taller	tallest
clever	cleverer	cleverest	narrow	narrower	narrowest
(b)		Different word for comparative and superlative			
bad	worse	worst	little	less	least
far	farther	farthest	many	more	most
good	better	best	much	more	most

Positive	Comparative	Superlative
(c)	Longer word in positive	
beautiful	more beautiful	most beautiful
careful	more careful	most careful
comfortable	more comfortable	most comfortable
ignorant	more ignorant	most ignorant

70

Comparison of Adjectives

1. Give the comparatives and superlatives of:

   many, hot, bad, famous, little.

2. Write the comparatives of:

   fast, good, gracious, tall, beautiful.

3. Write the superlatives of:

   thin, much, comfortable, gay, handsome.

4. Complete the following table:

Positive	Comparative	Superlative
long	longer	longest
far	....	....
good	....	....
generous	....	....
late	....	....
cautious	....	....

5. State whether the following words are positive, comparative or superlative:

   nearest, better, far, more certain, surest, larger, most wonderful, bad, shorter, biggest.

6. Correct the following sentences:
   (1) James was the biggest of the twins.
   (2) A more kinder lady you could not meet.
   (3) The best team won the football match.
   (4) Fred was the most fast of all the runners.
   (5) Who is the tallest, Jack or Betty?
   (6) He proved to be the ignorantest person.
   (7) Of the two, I like George best.
   (8) A badder boy I have never known.
   (9) The sailor lifted the thinnest end of the rope.
   (10) The patient made the wonderfulest recovery.

THE ADVERB

An **Adverb** is a word which modifies or adds to the meaning of a verb, an adjective, or another adverb.

Adverbs may be divided, according to their use, into the following classes:

(a) **TIME** — before, now, since, then, already, soon, seldom.
　　　Example: We have met **before**.

(b) **PLACE** — here, there, everywhere, nowhere.
　　　Example: They came **here** yesterday.

(c) **MANNER** — badly, easily, slowly, well.
　　　Example: The tall boy won **easily**.

(d) **DEGREE** — almost, much, only, quite, very, rather.
　　　Example: The old lady walked **very** slowly.

(e) **NUMBER** — once, twice.
　　　Example: They ran **twice** round the park.

(f) **QUESTIONING** — where, when, how.
　　　Example: When did you see him?

(g) **AFFIRMATION** and **NEGATION** — yes, certainly, no, not.
　　　Examples: She can **certainly** swim.
　　　　　　　I have **not** read the book.

(Many adverbs are often used as connecting words and therefore become conjunctions. You will read about them on page 89.)

NOTE — The majority of Adverbs are formed from corresponding Adjectives by adding "-ly", e.g.

quickly, bravely, seriously, happily, clearly, slowly, quietly, angrily, fatally, suitably.

EXERCISES

Underline the **Adverbs** in the following sentences:

1. Dinner will soon be ready.
2. There lay the object of our search.
3. The man walked slowly across the field.
4. The apples were quite good.
5. I once saw an eagle kill a rabbit.
6. Where did you find that knife?
7. He can certainly boast about his adventures.
8. We did not go to the concert.

Comparison of Adverbs

Adverbs are compared in the same way as **Adjectives.** As most adverbs are two-syllable words or longer they generally form the Comparative and Superlative by adding **"more"** and **"most"** to the Positive.

	Positive	Comparative	Superlative
Regular *(i)*			
	early	earlier	earliest
	fast	faster	fastest
	long	longer	longest
	soon	sooner	soonest
Regular *(ii)*			
	bitterly	more bitterly	most bitterly
	bravely	more bravely	most bravely
	briefly	more briefly	most briefly
	carefully	more carefully	most carefully
	clearly	more clearly	most clearly
	cruelly	more cruelly	most cruelly
	easily	more easily	most easily
	freely	more freely	most freely
	greedily	more greedily	most greedily
	happily	more happily	most happily
	loudly	more loudly	most loudly
	quickly	more quickly	most quickly
	slowly	more slowly	most slowly
	willingly	more willingly	most willingly
Irregular			
	badly	worse	worst
	far	farther	farthest
	forth	further	furthest
	ill	worse	worst
	late	later	last
	much	more	most
	well	better	best

Some Common Verbs with Suitable Adverbs

Verbs	Adverbs
acted	quickly, suddenly, warily.
answered	correctly, immediately, tartly.
ate	greedily, hungrily, quickly, slowly.
bled	freely, profusely, slightly.
bowed	humbly, respectfully, stiffly.
caressed	fondly, gently, lovingly.
charged	bravely, desperately, furiously.
chuckled	artfully, gleefully, happily
crept	quietly, silently, softly, stealthily.
decided	carefully, eventually, immediately.
explained	briefly, clearly, concisely, vaguely.
fell	heavily, quickly, suddenly.
flogged	brutally, cruelly, unmercifully.
fought	bravely, furiously, gamely.
frowned	angrily, sulkily, worriedly.
injured	accidentally, fatally, seriously, slightly.
left	hurriedly, quietly, suddenly.
listened	anxiously, attentively, carefully.
lost	badly, heavily, sportingly.
mumbled	angrily, inaudibly, indistinctly.
pondered	deeply, seriously, thoughtfully.
pulled	hastily, strongly, vigorously.
ran	hurriedly, quickly, rapidly, slowly.
remembered	clearly, distinctly, faintly, slightly.
sang	loudly, softly, sweetly, tunefully.
shone	brightly, brilliantly, clearly, dimly.
shouted	frantically, joyfully, jubilantly, loudly, suddenly.
slept	fitfully, lightly, soundly.
smiled	broadly, happily, ruefully.
sneered	insolently, impudently, tauntingly.
spent	foolishly, freely, recklessly, sparingly.
spoke	clearly, distinctly, earnestly, loudly, plainly, slowly.
sprang	hurriedly, lightly, quickly, suddenly.
staggered	awkwardly, drunkenly, weakly.
strove	bravely, desperately, manfully.
stuttered	excitedly, haltingly, painfully.
trembled	fearfully, frightfully, visibly.
waited	patiently, anxiously.

Some Common Verbs with Suitable Adverbs

Verbs	Adverbs
walked	clumsily, haltingly, quickly, slouchingly, slowly, smartly.
wept	bitterly, distractedly, sadly, touchingly.
whispered	audibly, quietly, softly.
yielded	stubbornly, weakly, willingly.

EXERCISES

1. In the spaces provided place the following adverbs:

   heavily, furiously, silently, soundly, immediately, sparingly, broadly, patiently.

He charged	....	He decided	....
He slept	....	He crept	....
He spent	....	He fell	....
He smiled	....	He waited	....

2. Add any suitable adverb to the following sentences:

The girl sings	....	The clerk wrote	....
The lion roars	....	The river flows	....
The artist paints	....	The stars shine	....
The child sleeps	....	The horse gallops	....
The cat walks	....	The man frowns	....

3. Give the comparatives and superlatives of:

   soon, briefly, well, early, clearly.

4. Write the comparatives of:

   long, badly, carefully, late, freely.

5. State the superlatives of:

   fast, quickly, ill, easily, forth.

6. Complete the following table:

Positive	Comparative	Superlative
long	....	....
happily	....	....
late	....	....
willingly	....	....
ill	....	....

WORD-BUILDING

Form Nouns from:

able	civilise	famous	magic	sad
absent	clean	favourite	manly	satisfy
abundant	collect	feed	marry	scene
accurate	commence	fierce	merry	school
acquaint	compare	fly	mission	scientific
act	conclude	fragrant	mock	secure
admire	confident	free	moral	see
adopt	confuse	friend	mountain	select
advertise	content	gay	move	serene
allow	create	grand	music	serve
amuse	credit	great	occupy	shade
angry	cruel	grow	oppose	sick
anxious	curious	hate	persuade	simple
appear	dark	hero	please	speak
applaud	deceive	high	proclaim	steal
apply	decent	holy	profess	stream
approve	decide	imagine	prosper	strike
arrive	deep	imitate	proud	strong
ascend	defend	inform	prove	succeed
assist	depart	injure	provide	superior
attend	describe	interfere	punctual	tell
attract	destroy	introduce	punish	think
bag	develop	invent	pursue	thrive
beautiful	discover	invite	ready	typical
beg	divide	judge	real	vain
begin	do	just	rebel	various
behave	encourage	know	receive	visit
believe	enjoy	laugh	recognise	war
bitter	enter	lazy	relieve	warm
boy	equal	learn	remember	weak
brave	exceed	like	renew	weary
breathe	exhaust	listen	repeat	weigh
bright	expect	live	repent	wide
cash	explain	long	resent	wise
child	faithful	lose	reveal	worthy
choose	false	loyal	revive	young

Form Adjectives from:

ability	critic	heat	notice	strength
accident	cruelty	height	oak	study
admire	custom	hero	obey	success
adventure	danger	hope	occasion	sun
affection	deceive	imagine	oppose	sympathy
angel	decide	industry	ornament	talk
anger	describe	inform	parent	terror
anxiety	destroy	introduce	patience	thirst
athlete	disaster	iron	peace	thought
attract	distance	Italy	peril	tide
autumn	duty	joy	person	tire
beauty	energy	law	picture	trouble
bible	enjoy	learn	pity	truth
boy	exceed	length	please	type
brass	expression	life	poet	union
breath	faith	love	poison	value
Britain	fame	luxury	pride	vanity
care	fashion	man	prosper	variety
caution	father	marvel	quarrel	victory
centre	fault	meddle	rag	voice
change	favour	melody	reason	volcano
charity	fire	mercy	science	Wales
child	five	metal	sense	war
choir	fool	mine	shadow	water
choose	force	mischief	shower	wave
circle	forget	mock	silk	weary
collect	fortune	mountain	silver	west
colony	France	mourn	sister	winter
comfort	friend	move	skill	wisdom
conclude	giant	music	sorrow	wit
continent	girl	mystery	south	wood
courage	gold	nation	spire	wool
coward	grace	nature	spirit	worth
craft	grief	neglect	star	wretch
credit	harm	noise	stop	year
crime	hate	north	storm	youth

Word-Building

Form Verbs from:

able	courage	frost	long	shelf
actor	creator	full	magnet	short
banishment	critic	glass	moisture	simple
bath	custom	glory	nation	soft
beauty	dark	gold	obedience	solution
blood	deed	grass	peril	song
bright	description	grief	pleasure	spark
broad	dictation	growth	proof	speech
camp	education	horror	provision	strong
circle	false	imitation	pure	success
circulation	fat	joy	relief	terror
civil	fertile	just	resident	thought
clean	fine	knee	resolution	tight
cloth	food	knowledge	rich	tomb
colony	force	large	roll	trial
composition	friend	life	sharp	wide

Form Adverbs from:

ability	happy	joy	sweet	true
critic	heavy	pure	terror	weary
faith	horror	simple	thought	wide

COMPOUND WORDS

A word in its simplest form is called a Primary Word, e.g. table, board, egg. If we combine two Primary Words to form one word we get a Compound Word, e.g. tablecloth, blackboard, eggcup.

Form Compound Words from the following:

ache	cup	guard	maid	pot	strong
ball	day	gun	man	room	table
black	door	hat	master	safe	tea
board	dust	heart	mat	school	time
boot	egg	house	milk	servant	tomb
cart	fall	jam	mill	shed	tooth
church	fire	lace	out	shop	thrift
cloth	fly	lamp	pick	son	water
coal	foot	life	piece	spend	wife
craft	gentle	light	pond	stand	witch
cry	grand	load	post	stone	yard

Word-Building

EXERCISES

1. Make a noun corresponding to each of the following words:

please	....	encourage	....
prove	....	strong	....
know	....	real	....
proud	....	just	....
choose	....	give	....

2. Give nouns formed from:

gay, select, grow, bag, act, receive, invite, succeed, repent, divide.

3. By adding a suffix, form a noun from each of the following:

astonish, coward, critic, trick, assist, free, inform, loyal, invent, sick.

4. Make an adjective corresponding to each of the following words:

Britain, heat, expense, anger, faith, height, fashion, boy, vanity, sense.

5. Give adjectives from:

decide	....	mystery	....
bible	....	voice	....
talk	....	nation	....
circle	....	winter	....
attract	....	peril	....

6. Give a verb corresponding to each of the following words:

Example: Solution — **solve**.

knee	....	tight	....
strong	....	grief	....
description	....	large	....
gold	....	glory	....
custom	....	food	....

7. Give verbs from:

obedient, sweet, education, fat, life, composition, civil, tomb, bath, pure.

Word-Building

8. Form adverbs from:

   anger, tune, excitement, freedom, anxiety, frantic, worry, serious, fool, silence.

9. Complete the following compound words:

............board	milk............	grand............
hat............	............cup	............post
lamp............	............cloth	............ball
tooth............	book............	............stool

10. Complete the following table:

Adjective	Noun	Verb
long	length	lengthen
strong	....	....
broad	....	....
glad	....	....
able	....	....
wide	....	....

11. Make sentences, two for each word, using the following words *(a)* as nouns; *(b)* as adjectives:

    brick, chief, diamond, garden, iron, light, music, shilling, sole, square, summer, young.

12. Write sentences, two for each word, using each of the following words — first as a noun and then as a verb:

    brush, cycle, fire, heat, hope, notice, sail, saw, spring, step, turn, wave.

13. What part of speech is the word **round** in each of the following sentences?

    (1) It was a large **round** table.   ....
    (2) The tourist played a **round** of golf.   ....
    (3) The speaker turned **round**.   ....
    (4) The boy ran quickly **round** the field.   ....
    (5) The horses must **round** this corner.   ....

CONCORD

Concord means agreement or harmony. In grammar we apply this word as meaning perfect agreement between subject and verb. This is shown by the subject and verb having the same person and number.

(a) When the **subject** is **singular**, the **verb** is **singular**, e.g.

    (1) He writes.   (2) She swims.   (3) The baby cries.

(b) When the **subject** is **plural**, the **verb** is **plural**, e.g.

    (1) We write.   (2) They swim.   (3) The babies cry.

(c) Expressions such as **"each of"**, **"one of"**, **"neither of"**, **"every one of"**, **"not one of"** and words such as **"each"**, **"every"**, **"none"**, **"anybody"**, **"everybody"** and **"nobody"** must be followed by **verbs** in the **singular**, e.g.

    (1) **Each of** the boys **has** a toy.
    (2) **One of** the ladies **is** married.
    (3) **Neither of** the brothers **was** present.
    (4) **Is either of** the sisters coming?
    (5) **Every one of** us **knows** that it is wrong.
    (6) **Not one of** the girls **has** a skipping rope.
    (7) **Each** man **was** searched.
    (8) **Every** child **has** a secret ambition.
    (9) **Anybody is** admitted to the caves.
    (10) **Everybody was** delighted at the close.
    (11) **Nobody is** displeased with the result.
    (12) **None** of the ships **was** lost.

(d) A **singular subject** with attached phrases introduced by **"with"** or **"like"** or **"as well as"** is followed by a **singular verb,** e.g.

    (1) The boy, **with** several others, **was** late for school.
    (2) Alice, **like** Rose, **is** tall for her age.
    (3) Tom, **as well as** Fred, **rises** early in the morning.

(e) When a **verb** has **two singular subjects** connected by **"and"**, the **verb** is **plural**, e.g.

    (1) The cat **and** the dog **were** great friends.
    (2) The farmer **and** his wife **are** jolly people.

Concord

(f)   When a **verb** has **one or more plural subjects** connected by **"and"**, the verb is **plural**, e.g.

(1)   The officer **and** his men **were** crossing the field.

(2)   The boys **and** the girls **are** sure of their work.

(g)   **Two singular subjects** separated by **"either** .... **or"**, **"neither** .... **nor"** take a **singular verb**, e.g.

(1)   **Either** one **or** the other **has** blundered.

(2)   **Either** he **or** she **is** right.

(3)   **Neither** Grace **nor** Helen **knows** anything about it.

(4)   **Neither** he **nor** she **writes** well.

(h)   **Subjects** separated by **"either** *(plural)* **or"**, **"neither** *(plural)* **nor"**, **"both** .... **and"**, also **"all** .... **but"**, take a **plural verb**, e.g.

(1)   **Either** the boys **or** the girls **are** to blame.

(2)   **Neither** the pirates **nor** the sailors **were** afraid of battle.

(3)   **Both** Hugh **and** Sam **were** standing.

(4)   **All but** James **are** going to the picnic.

(5)   **All of** them **but** Grace **are** correct.

EXERCISES

In each of the sentences below there are groups of two words within brackets. One of the two words is correct, the other wrong. Underline the correct word:

Each of the boys (is, are) going on holiday so each of them (has, have) gone to bed early.

Everybody (was, were) pleased as each of them (was, were) treated alike.

Neither he nor she (want, wants) to go.

(Wasn't, Weren't) we sorry when we heard you (was, were) going?

One of the men (is, are) married and so he (get, gets) preference.

All but William (has, have) behaved well so all but William (get, gets) away early.

James as well as John (rise, rises) at eight, so James like John (is, are) early for work.

Neither of the singers (was, were) present.

Every little girl (desire, desires) a nice doll.

The miller and his wife (is, are) a happy couple.

Why (does, do) every one of us (do, does) stupid things at times?

Neither of them (has, have) failed as both of them (is, are) right in five sums.

The girl with several others (was, were) going to school.

Both Agnes and Albert (is, are) here tonight.

Either Fred or Jean (has, have) made a mistake so either he or she (is, are) wrong.

Not one of the boys (has, have) a knife although not one of the boys (is, are) young.

John like James (is, are) smaller than Peter.

(Is, Are) Frank and Margaret happy, as both he and she (was, were) complaining?

All of you but Andrew (is, are) good, so all of you but Andrew (get, gets) a reward.

Each of the ladies (is, are) delighted as each of the ladies (receive, receives) a prize.

Anybody (is, are) allowed to enter.

Every one of us (know, knows) the answers because every one of us (was, were) copying.

Nobody (is, are) grumpy at the camp because nobody (is, are) allowed to feel lonely.

Arthur as well as Donald (is, are) clever so Arthur as well as Donald (has, have) succeeded.

The gentlemen and the ladies (was, were) wearing evening dress.

Either one or the other (is, are) wealthy as either one or the other (has, have) plenty of money.

All of us but David (was, were) on holiday so all of us but David (is, are) sun-tanned.

(Wasn't, Weren't) they pleased when they heard we (was, were) coming?

Cecil as well as Annie (like, likes) spelling and Cecil as well as Annie (hate, hates) arithmetic.

Either Flora or Richard (has, have) measles, so either she or he (is, are) in bed.

Why (do, does) every one of them do that, when every one of them (know, knows) the arrangements?

THE PRONOUN

There are **Personal, Relative, Interrogative, Demonstrative** and **Indefinite** Pronouns. Pronouns stand **for** (pro-) nouns.

The Personal Pronouns and some of the Relative and Interrogative Pronouns have a **Nominative** form when they are the subject of a verb, an **Objective** form when they are the object of a verb (or preposition) and a **Possessive** form. Personal pronouns also distinguish the **First Person** (the person(s) speaking, i.e. I or we), the **Second Person** (the person(s) spoken to, i.e. you) and the **Third Person** (the person(s) spoken about). So we have:

Personal Pronouns:

Person	Nominative	Objective	Possessive	Reflexive	(Possessive Adjective)
First (Sing.)	I	me	mine	myself	(my), (mine*)
Second (Sing.)	thou*	thee*	thine*	thyself*	(thy*), (thine*)
	you	you	yours	yourself	(your)
Third (Sing.)	he	him	his	himself	(his)
	she	her	hers	herself	(her)
	it	it	its	itself	(its)
First (Plur.)	we	us	ours	ourselves	(our)
Second (Plur.)	you	you	yours	yourselves	(your)
Third (Plur.)	they	them	theirs	themselves	(their)

* These forms are little used in modern English.

Note 1. The reflexive form is used in two ways *(a)* reflexive, *(b)* intensive, e.g.
> I have cut myself. He blames himself. (Reflexive.)
> I myself was unaware of that. (Intensive, emphatic.)

Note 2. The reflexives do not have different forms for nominative, objective or possessive. It is wrong to say *hisself* or *theirselves*.

Note 3. A *possessive adjective* simply describes a noun, e.g. *your* pencil.
> The *possessive of a pronoun* stands for a noun, e.g.
> This pencil is *yours* (i.e. *your pencil*).
> He's a friend of *ours* (i.e. from among *our friends*).

Nominative and **Objective** forms — correct use.

The **nominative** forms of pronouns must be used for subjects of verbs.

I bought some apples.	*We* saw a large cave.
You will catch a cold.	*They* shouted with joy.
He caught a fish.	*She* sang a song.

The objective forms must be used for objects of verbs or prepositions.

> The play bored *me*.
>
> The animal stared *at me*.

> The children left *us*.
>
> Go and run *after them*.

Special case — Complement of the verb *to be*.

The verb *to be* does not take an object. When we say "That is nonsense", the word *nonsense* is called the complement (or 'completion') of the verb *is*.

> It *is I* who am the master of my fate   (*I* is the complement of *is*).
>
> It *was they*, not *we*, who ran away   (*they*, *we* complements of *was*).

Mistakes are common when *that* is used for *who*, e.g.

> It was *them*, not *us*, *that* ran away (wrong).

In the first sentence we could even have two mistakes:

> It is *me* that *is* the master of my fate (*me*, *is*, both wrong).

Exception: If someone asks "Who is there?" the answer "It is *me*" is now accepted in practice, though "It is I" is the grammatically correct form.

Note: It is not only the simple parts of the verb *to be* which have a complement, e.g.

> It *appears to be they* who are refusing.

Double Nominatives and Objectives.

The above rules — **nominative for the subject** (and for the complement of the verb *to be*), **objective for the object** (of a verb or preposition) — apply also where there is more than one subject or object, e.g. two pronouns, or a noun and a pronoun.

Examples:

> *She* and *I* can't agree.
>
> It's *you* and *I* who lose.

> It suits both *them* and *us*.
>
> Between *you* and *me*, he's mad.

Errors:

> It's *you* and *me* who lose.

> Between *you* and *I*, he's mad.

Other Errors to Avoid

(a)   After *as* and *than*.

> (Wrong.) He is as tall as me.
>
> (Wrong.) He is taller than me.

> (Correct.) He is as tall as *I* (am).
>
> (Correct.) He is taller than *I* (am).

Note these sentences, however:

> She likes you as much as *me*.   ⎫
>
> She likes you more than *me*.   ⎬

> Both correct. Means "as much as (more than) she likes *me*".

> She likes you as much as *I*.   ⎫
>
> She likes you more than *I*.   ⎬

> Both correct. Means "as much as (more than) I like you".

The Pronoun

(b)   *Spelling* of *its* (pronoun) and *it's*.

Its is the possessive of *it* (strangely, with no apostrophe).
e.g. This class has forgotten *its* manners.

It's stands for *it is* (or *it has*). The apostrophe denotes omissions.
e.g. *It's* dry today, but *it's* been wet recently.

Relative Pronouns. A relative pronoun (*who*, *whom*, *whose*, *which*, *what*, *that*) joins two parts of a sentence, standing in one part for a noun or pronoun mentioned in the other part, and referring to that noun or pronoun, which is called its **antecedent**, e.g.

Tom is a boy *who* learns fast.	That's a job *of which* I'm proud.
She is a pupil *whom* I taught.	This is the house *that* Jack built.
Was it he *whose* boat sank?	*What* is to be, will be.

Sometimes a relative pronoun is omitted and has to be 'understood', e.g.

That's a girl ↑ I taught last year.   The shop ↑ I went to was shut.

Sometimes the pronoun includes its own antecedent, e.g.

Who steals my purse steals trash	(*who = he, who* . . . . . .)
What will be, will be	(*what = that, which* . . . . . .)

Who, *whom* refer only to persons (singular or plural)

who, the nominative, must be used only for the subject of a verb,

whom, the objective, must always be used for the object of a verb or preposition, e.g. Is there anyone *whom* we can trust?
It is wrong to say: Is there anyone *who* we can trust?

Whose, *that* can refer to persons, animals or things, singular or plural,

Which is used to refer to animals and things (singular or plural) but not to persons. Its possessive form is either *whose* or *of which*.

What is seldom used as a relative pronoun, though it is common as an interrogative. It is sometimes wrongly used instead of *that*, e.g.

This is the book *what* I lost (wrong).
This is the book *that* I lost (correct).

The Pronoun

Interrogative Pronouns (*who? whom? whose? which? what?*) ask a question. They refer to persons, animals and things just as when used as relative pronouns.

It is a common mistake to use *who?* (the nominative form) in sentences where *whom?* (the objective) is required, e.g.

> *Who* do you think I met? (wrong).
> *Whom* do you think I met? (*Whom* is the object of *met*) (correct).

N.B. *Who* do you think you are? is correct. (*Are* is part of the verb *to be*, which does not take an object.)

Demonstrative Pronouns (*this, that, these, those*) 'point out' what they stand for, e.g.

This is intolerable.	I like *that*.	He is like *that* sometimes.
I prefer *these* to *those*.	*That's* better.	Is it as serious as *that*?

Note 1. *This* and *these*, when opposed to *that* and *those* in a sentence, usually distinguish what is nearer, more recent, or more recently mentioned, from what is more distant in place or time, e.g.

> *That* was nonsense: the truth is *this* . . . . . .

Note 2. The words *this, that, these, those* are, of course, also used as (demonstrative) adjectives, when they point out *and* describe a noun in a sentence, or one that is understood, e.g.

> *This* house is bigger than *that* (house).
> *That* is the wrong door. (*door* is understood after *that*.)

Indefinite Pronouns stand for some person(s) or thing(s) unspecified, e.g.

Tell me *more*.	You don't know *much*.	*Both* owned up.
Either will do.	*One* must remember.	*None* returned.
Take *any* of them.	Give me a black *one*; I dislike white *ones*.	

Note 1. A singular indefinite pronoun must not be referred to as if it were a plural. This is a very common error, e.g.

> *Everyone* must pay *their* fair share (wrong).
> *Everyone* must pay *his* fair share (correct).
> *Everyone* must pay *his* or *her* fair share (correct).

Note 2. Another common error is to switch from the indefinite *one* to another pronoun, e.g.

> *One* must not miss *his* chance (wrong).
> *One* must not miss *one's* chance (correct).

The Pronoun

Complete these sentences using the correct word from each pair in brackets:

1. (He, Him) and (I, me) went for a walk.
2. It was (he, him) (who, whom) we saw in the shop.
3. No one believes it was (she, her); everyone thinks it was (I, me).
4. Between (he, him) and (I, me) we ate the whole cake.
5. (She, Her) and (I, me) can go, but you and (he, him) cannot.
6. Jack is not as clever as (he, him) or (I, me).
7. It seems to be (they, them) (who, whom) the police suspect.
8. (Her, She) and you sang very well together.
9. John is much brighter than (he, him) or (I, me).
10. This discovery must remain a secret between you and (I, me).
11. It's not for (we, us) to run after (they, them).
12. It was (he, him) who knew the right answer.
13. (Who, Whom) are (they, them)?
14. (We, Us) lads were at the cinema at the same time as (they, them).
15. Between you and (I, me), I know all about Sue and (she, her).
16. He is almost as big as (I, me) but smaller than (she, her).
17. Her sisters are smaller than (we, us) but she is taller than (I, me).
18. You must choose between (they, them) and (we, us).
19. You and (I, we) could do it, but not you and (he, him).
20. It appears to be (she, her) about (who, whom) you should worry.
21. (She, Her) and (I, me) are twelve years of age.
22. Her cousin is younger than (she, her) or (I, me).
23. Was it (I, me) (who, whom) you saw there?
24. I spoke to (he, him) and (she, her) about (who, whom) to tell.
25. We are certain it was not (he, him) (who, whom) was to blame.
26. It is not (she, her) that I am angry with, but (he, him).
27. (He, Him) I can excuse, but not (they, them).
28. Was it (he, him) or (she, her) who found the purse?
29. (Who, Whom) do you think we met?
30. Anyone (who's, whose) poor shouldn't buy one of (them, these).
31. That's not your pencil. (Its, It's) (mine, mine's).
32. Everyone (what, that) wants a ticket, must bring (their, his) money.
33. Neither he nor she (know, knows) what (they, he or she) (is, are) doing.
34. Let's go, you and (I, me), and see (who's, whose) (there, their).
35. (Who, Whom) were you speaking to?

THE CONJUNCTION

A Conjunction joins words, phrases or sentences together.

There are two main kinds of conjunction:

(a) **Conjunctions which join similar parts of speech and clauses of equal value,** e.g.

and, both .... and, but, for, whereas, either .... or, neither .... nor.

Examples:

(1) The boy **and** the girl hurried home.
(2) The dog was delighted with the bone **and** wagged his tail.
(3) **Both** he **and** his wife went on holiday.
(4) **Both** the driver **and** the man, who was hurt, were questioned.
(5) He was poor **but** honest.
(6) She could write well, **but** she could not do her sums.
(7) I gave him the money, **for** he had earned it.
(8) I am surprised at him **for** he should know better.
(9) He worked hard, **whereas** I did very little.
(10) He thought himself wealthy, **whereas** he was poor.
(11) **Either** my brother **or** his chum knows the place.
(12) **Either** my nephew goes with me **or** he stays at home.
(13) **Neither** James **nor** Mary wants to go.
(14) **Neither** did he come **nor** did he send any excuse.

(b) **Conjunctions which join principal clauses to subordinate clauses**. (Included are many adverbs which act as connecting words and therefore become conjunctions.) In order to distinguish the various types of conjunction in this class they are grouped under the appropriate headings below:

TIME

Conjunctions are:

after, before, since, until, till, when, whenever, while, now, that, as.

Examples:

(1) **After** the lady opened the door she switched on the light.
(2) The man ate a sandwich **before** he boarded the bus.
(3) **Since** I have known her we have been firm friends.

The Conjunction

    (4) We will wait here **until** the next train arrives.

    (5) I cannot say definitely **till** I hear from him.

    (6) The boys were going to school **when** we saw them.

    (7) **Whenever** it is possible we shall visit her.

    (8) **While** there is life there is hope.

    (9) **Now that** we have finished, let us go home.

   (10) **As** I was on my way home, I fell.

PLACE

Conjunctions are:

    whence, where, wherever, whither.

Examples:

    (1) He looked back **whence** he had come.

    (2) Put it **where** he cannot see it.

    (3) The brooch must be found **wherever** it is.

    (4) **Whither** thou goest, I will go.

CAUSE or REASON

Conjunctions are:

    as, because, lest, since.

Examples:

    (1) **As** he was in a hurry I did not speak to him.

    (2) We know he was to blame **because** we saw the accident.

    (3) I was afraid **lest** he should fall.

    (4) Do not say anything **since** she is frightened.

CONCESSION

Conjunctions are:

    although, even if, though, whether .... or, while, as.

Examples:

    (1) **Although** I have written twice, he has not replied.

    (2) I would not go **even if** I were invited.

    (3) **Though** the boy had faults I could not but like him.

    (4) It is the truth **whether** you believe it **or** not.

    (5) **While** we should condemn vice, we should praise virtue.

    (6) He could not get the answer, clever **as** he was.

CONDITION

Conjunctions are:

except that, if, unless.

Examples:

    (1) **Except that** she is a trifle slow, she writes well.

    (2) Send me word **if** you wish to go.

    (3) That rascal will do nothing **unless** he is compelled.

MANNER or DEGREE

Conjunctions are:

as, as .... as, as if, as though, so .... as, than.

Examples:

    (1) He remained at home **as** he had been ordered.

    (2) The house is vacant **as** far **as** we know.

    (3) He speaks **as if** he knows all about it.

    (4) The animal lay **as though** it were dead.

    (5) James does not read **so** well **as** Robert.

    (6) He is taller **than** I am.

PURPOSE

Conjunctions are:

in order that, lest, so that, that.

Examples:

    (1) They worked hard **in order that** they might finish in time.

    (2) Take care, **lest** you are hurt.

    (3) I sent him a letter **so that** he would know.

    (4) You come to school **that** you may learn.

CONSEQUENCE

Conjunctions are:

so that, so .... that.

Examples:

    (1) The man spoke loudly **so that** he was easily heard.

    (2) She is **so** dull **that** she can learn nothing.

The Conjunction

In the following exercises there are sentences with groups of two words within brackets. One of the two words is correct, the other wrong. Underline the correct word:

TIME

(1) Wait there (how, till) I have finished.
(2) He left (before, that) darkness fell.
(3) We have remained here (whether, since) you left.
(4) (After, Unless) they arrived, they sat down.
(5) I can call (however, whenever) it is convenient to you.
(6) The exercise will be corrected (before, when) it is finished.
(7) His brother waited (except, until) James returned.
(8) She read a book (that, while) I wrote a letter.
(9) (Now that, Unless) the weather has changed the farmers can expect good crops.
(10) (Until, As) he went up the stairs, he stumbled.

PLACE

(1) He went (whence, unless) he could not return.
(2) The faithful dog followed his master (lest, wherever) he went.
(3) There were many trees (since, where) I sat down.
(4) They followed (whither, than) he led them.

CAUSE or REASON

(1) (As, Where) we left early, we did not see him.
(2) I was afraid to speak (lest, however) he should tell.
(3) You ask him (since, than) you are friends.
(4) My uncle was angry (where, because) he was deceived.

CONCESSION

(1) The boy is strong and healthy (though, since) he is not tall.
(2) (While, Unless) I trust him, I dislike his companions.
(3) We will go (how, even if) it rains.
(4) (Whether, Where) you like it or not, he will invite you.
(5) My cold is much worse (although, whence) I have tried to cure it.

The Conjunction

CONDITION

(1) (Except that, Unless) he is sometimes nervous, he manages quite well.
(2) She will go (than, if) you ask her.
(3) You cannot obtain admission (unless, since) you pay.

MANNER or DEGREE

(1) You are quite right (while, as far as) I can see.
(2) The dog lifted his paw (as though, how) he understood me.
(3) She is older (than, since) I am.
(4) They did not play (while, so well as) their opponents.
(5) The man looked (when, as if) he was a foreigner.
(6) I cannot work (as, whence) he can.

PURPOSE

(1) The man put on the light (so that, since) he could read.
(2) (In order that, When) they might be in time, they left early.
(3) The boy ran quickly (why, lest) he should be left behind.
(4) You should go (that, how) you may be cured.

CONSEQUENCE

(1) The dog ran so fast (that, while) he caught the hare.
(2) He ran quickly (when, so that) he was in time for tea.

THE PREPOSITION

The Preposition is placed before (pre) a noun or a pronoun. It defines a relationship to the noun or pronoun.

The following list contains the most common prepositions:

> about, above, across, after, against, along, amid, amidst, among, amongst, around, at, before, behind, below, beneath, beside, between, betwixt, beyond, by, down, during, except, for, from, in, into, near, of, off, on, over, round, since, through, till, to, towards, under, underneath, until, unto, up, upon, with, within, without.

1. Use the correct prepositions in the blank spaces:

    (1) The boy must apologise .... the lady.

    (2) That man is an authority .... flowers.

    (3) The mother was proud .... her son's success.

    (4) He placed the bat .... the wall.

    (5) My cousin put the book .... the drawer.

    (6) It is an exception .... the rule.

    (7) His opinion differs .... mine.

    (8) The man ran .... the path.

    (9) She takes great pride .... her appearance.

   (10) The ball went .... the window.

2. Supply three suitable prepositions in each sentence:

    (1) The pencil lay
        ....
        .... the desk.
        ....

    (2) The man rowed
        ....
        .... the river.
        ....

    (3) The lady sat
        ....
        .... the chairman.
        ....

3. Underline the prepositions in the following sentences:

    (1) I stood on the bridge of the ship.

    (2) Above me, I saw a cloudy sky.

    (3) The dog leaped over the wall after a ball.

    (4) We chased him through a field of hay.

    (5) With that ticket you can obtain admission to the show.

(6) My brother received a letter from him.
(7) The farmer stored his hay in a large barn.
(8) Beside the boxes lay several boulders.
(9) The careless boy ran behind the car.
(10) During the year many people were injured in street accidents.

Many people find it difficult to choose the correct prepositions. The following should be read carefully and revised from time to time:

according to	filled with
afflict with	full of
agree to (something)	good for
agree with (somebody)	guilty of
aim at	indignant at (something)
angry at (something)	indignant with (somebody)
angry with (somebody)	inspired by
ashamed of	interfere with
attack on	invasion of
blame for	meddle with
change for (something)	opposite to
change with (somebody)	part from (somebody)
comment on	part with (something)
compared with	prevail on
complain of	protest against
confer with	pursuit of
conscious of	recoil from
defiance of	regard for
despair of	rely on
die of	similar to
differ from (opinion)	suffer from
differ with (somebody)	tired of (something)
disagree with	tired with (action)
disappointed in (something)	thirst for (or after)
disappointed with (somebody)	vexed at (something)
disgusted at (something)	vexed with (somebody)
disgusted with (somebody)	victim of
dislike for	wait for (person, thing)
divide among (many)	wait upon (somebody)
divide between (two)	write about (something)
equal to	write to (somebody)

CORRECTION OF SENTENCES

There are errors in the following sentences. Rewrite them correctly.

1. She was the oldest of the two sisters.
2. Who did you see at the party?
3. Neither John or James were present.
4. She is not as old as me.
5. The best team won the football match.
6. The books what we read were interesting.
7. Being a fine day I went to the seashore.
8. Who can it be for?
9. He was angry at me for leaving.
10. I am your's truly.
11. I cannot run no farther.
12. John has broke his leg.
13. Hurrah shouted the man.
14. The letter was sent to Mr. John Brown, Esq.
15. The parcel was returned back to the sender.
16. I left home at $\frac{1}{4}$ to 7.
17. The girl said that she done it herself.
18. He returned home as quick as he could.
19. I have forgot to post the letter.
20. "Where is my Boots?"
21. She hurted her leg.
22. She got a bad accident.
23. There is four books on the table.
24. He went for to get up.
25. The lady bought a comb for the baby with plastic teeth.
26. Between you and I, he is quite wrong.
27. They sung the same song twice.
28. This jacket is wore out.
29. It's no use me working.
30. I intended to have written.
31. I was that tired I could hardly of spoken.
32. The fishermen saw a flock of herring in the sea.
33. Immediately he ran to the injured man
34. Between you and me we seen many people.
35. I saw a dog with his master which had a long tail.
36. We found the ring belonging to the lady made of gold.
37. A piano was sold to a lady with carved legs.
38. We seen the rascal who stole were ball.
39. There is five books on the table.

40. A man was at the corner and his dog.
41. She and her husband am going.
42. His hair needs cutting badly.
43. Neither of them are tall.
44. Someone's left their books behind.
45. Him and his sister went to the pictures.
46. Me and my friend went to buy a coat for ourselves.
47. It was him you saw.
48. They have did it again.
49. She could not come no quicker.
50. We have never seen none of them.
51. He couldn't remember nothing.
52. He done his work correctly.
53. Is he the tallest of the two?
54. Each of the boys had their books.
55. It was me that broke the window.
56. Which is the cleverest, John or Mary?
57. A more kinder man never lived.
58. I was that breathless I could hardly speak.
59. The animal did not take no notice.
60. Neither of them have been lucky.
61. Me and him went together to the pictures.
62. He took the biggest half.
63. It was a remarkable fine picture.
64. He is worse than me.
65. I seen him go to the theatre.
66. One of the horses were tired.
67. Of the two, I like James best.
68. Give me them oranges.
69. He don't speak very clear.
70. We are quite sure he done it.
71. She sent it to you and I.
72. The man learnt him to swim.
73. That answer is different with mine.
74. Neither one or the other is right.
75. She will not stay, I do not think.
76. The lady sings quite nice.
77. He did not except the gift.
78. To who does this belong?
79. The child rose up from the floor.
80. The two brothers divided the apple among them.

THE RIGHT WORD IN THE RIGHT PLACE

1. Place the following words in the sentences best suited to their use:
   closed, finished, stopped, completed, concluded, ended.
   - (a) His watch .... at six o'clock.
   - (b) I remember how the story ....
   - (c) I have .... my lessons.
   - (d) They have .... the alterations.
   - (e) The meeting .... with the National Anthem.
   - (f) Having enough money they .... the fund.

2. Explain the difference between:
   learning — teaching, looking — staring, mumbling — bawling, striding — galloping, taking — snatching, tapping — battering, throwing — hurling, writing — scribbling.

3. Use the following words (instead of **"nice"**) to describe:
   agreeable, beautiful, convenient, delicious, enjoyable, fine, good, interesting, pleasant, pretty.

a .... garden	a .... bonnet	a .... cake
a .... walk	a .... house	an .... man
a .... day	a .... train	an .... concert
an .... book		

4. Place the following words in the sentences best suited to them:
   frowned, mumbled, sang, chuckled, bowed, whispered, listened, smiled.

He .... tunefully	He .... gleefully
He .... angrily	He .... broadly
He .... humbly	He .... attentively
He .... indistinctly	He .... softly

5. Place the following words in the sentences best suited to their use:
   exclaimed, muttered, answered, said, shouted, explained, whispered, pleaded.

He .... that he would come	He .... with joy
He .... why he was late	"Look!" he ....
He .... for mercy	He .... under his breath
He .... quietly to his neighbour	"That is so," he ....

The Right Word in the Right Place

6. Place the following words in the sentences best suited to them:
   caressed, ate, pulled, charged, slept, bled, crept, strove.

   He .... furiously.   He .... greedily.
   He .... profusely.   He .... soundly.
   He .... vigorously.   He .... manfully.
   He .... fondly.   He .... stealthily.

7. **Always avoid use of the word "got". There is usually another word which can be used to better effect.**

   Substitute a better word in each of the following sentences:
   (a) He **got up** at eight o'clock.
   (b) He **got** a penny from his mother.
   (c) He **got** his breakfast early.
   (d) He **got** a bad cold yesterday.
   (e) He **got to** the station in time.
   (f) He **got** married last year.

8. Write in the most suitable word:
   (a) A man who digs for coal is a ....
   (b) I switched on the .... light.
   (c) The .... holiday is in December.
   (d) They sang a Christmas ....
   (e) He was so ill .... he went to bed.
   (f) The postman .... the letters.
   (g) He avoided accidents because he drove very ....

9. Place the right words (from **who, whom, whose, which**) in the following sentences:
   (a) That is the boy .... broke the window.
   (b) That is the stone .... broke the window.
   (c) That is the man .... window was broken.
   (d) That is the boy .... I saw breaking the window.
   (e) That is the boy .... told me that he broke the window.

10. Words ending in "**-able**":
    (a) A piece of furniture.   *(f)* A telegram from oversea
    (b) A horse's home.   *(g)* Helpless.
    (c) Written by Æsop.   *(h)* Land under cultivation.
    (d) Can be carried.   *(i)* A carrot.
    (e) Diamonds are.   *(j)* Glass things are.

The Right Word in the Right Place

11. Give a single word for each of the following:

        (a) go away,   *(b)* go back,   *(c)* go down,   *(d)* go forward,

        (e) go into,   *(f)* go on hands and knees,   *(g)* go out of,

        (h) go quickly, *(i)* go slowly,   *(j)* go up.

12. Place the right words (from **no, not, never, none, any**) in the following sentences:

    (1) Did you notice .... friends there?

    (2) .... have I seen such a display.

    (3) We have .... received .... of the books.

    (4) .... thank you, I .... smoke.

    (5) We are .... going there .... more.

    (6) .... of the boys knew the answer.

    (7) ...., he is .... well enough to eat .... cakes.

    (8) Have you .... marbles? .... I have ....

13. From the following lengths choose the correct one for each sentence:

    two millimetres; fifteen centimetres; thirty centimetres; one hundred and eighty centimetres; four metres; seventy metres; six hundred and forty-three kilometres; four thousand eight hundred and twenty-seven kilometres.

    (1) The soldier was .... tall.

    (2) My exercise book is .... broad.

    (3) The height of the factory chimney was ....

    (4) The distance from London to Glasgow is about ....

    (5) The twine on the parcel was .... thick.

    (6) The distance from Southampton to New York is about ....

    (7) The room was .... high.

    (8) My ruler is .... long.

14. Explain the difference between:

    yacht — steamer,   motor — aeroplane,   river — canal, pen — pencil, shoes — boots, chair — sofa, pin — needle, tramcar — omnibus,   shadow — reflection,   clock — watch, ham — bacon, hay — straw, cigar — cheroot, kipper — herring, map — plan, ceiling — roof, picture — sketch.

The Right Word in the Right Place

15. There are a great many words to describe different ways of walking. For example: A hunter **walked** over the hills. A better word here would be **roved** or **roamed.** In the sentences below replace the word **walked** by a more suitable word from the following list. Any word once used may not be used again, so be careful and **watch your step**:

limped, strode, sneaked, toddled, paced, rambled, tramped, shuffled, plodded, strutted, strolled, stamped, hobbled, marched, sauntered, prowled.

(1) The nature lover **walked** through the woods.
(2) The lame man **walked** across the floor.
(3) The happy couple **walked** down the lane.
(4) The daring knight **walked** into the hall.
(5) The tourist **walked** through the art gallery.
(6) The soldiers **walked** to the station.
(7) Captain Smith **walked** up and down the deck.
(8) The cunning thief **walked** into the room.
(9) The baby **walked** across the floor.
(10) Proud Mr. Brown **walked** on to the platform.
(11) The weary farmer **walked** homewards.
(12) A gouty old man **walked** down the stairs.
(13) The hikers **walked** many a long mile.
(14) The angry man **walked** into his office.
(15) The burglar **walked** through the house.
(16) The sick patient **walked** over to the table.

16. The following may be said to be **the right action at the right time.** Tell what immediate action you would take and suggest a cure (if necessary). What would you do?

(1) If you burned your foot.
(2) If you lost your way.
(3) If you sprained your ankle.
(4) If your nose started to bleed.
(5) If you noticed an escape of gas in the house.
(6) If your sister's dress caught fire.
(7) If you found a pocket-book in the street.
(8) If your brother's hand was cut.
(9) If you saw smoke coming from a closed shop.
(10) If your cousin was stung in the arm.

ADDITION OF CLAUSES

Add a clause to the following and name the kind of clause you add:

1. I saw the lady ....
2. The little boy said ....
3. The girl ran quickly ....
4. .... when they reached home.
5. I noticed .... when he rose to speak.
6. We stood on the very spot ....
7. .... if you cannot swim.
8. The dog barked loudly ....
9. The lady .... was my sister.
10. "Will you let me know .... ?"
11. The dog .... saved the child.
12. We saw the train ....
13. I hope ....
14. .... while they listened.
15. The boy hurt himself badly ....
16. The man .... was caught by the police.
17. I saw ....
18. She bought an umbrella ....
19. .... as she spoke.
20. The messenger arrived ....
21. I watched the man ....
22. I do not know ....
23. As the girl approached the house ....
24. We saw .... when we returned.
25. .... if you are ill.
26. "Come to my house .... "
27. I know the child ....
28. When I came here ....
29. .... which cost twopence.
30. My father scolded me ....
31. The crowd rushed forward ....
32. The soldiers .... were trapped in the wood.
33. The unhappy scholar said ....
34. .... if you do not send word.
35. The boy lifted the box ....
36. The man waved frantically ....

REPLACEMENT

Change the underlined phrases into clauses:

1. He failed through carelessness.
2. On the completion of his task the boy went out to play.
3. He told me of his coming.
4. A man in high position has many responsibilities.
5. She lived in a cottage near the sea.
6. On entering I saw several pictures.
7. The police recovered the stolen property.
8. I was pleased to hear of his success.
9. We do not know his hiding place.
10. The roads leading to the fair were crowded.

Change the underlined clauses into phrases:

1. I am convinced that he is sincere.
2. The child was in bed before the sun had set.
3. His action showed how brave he was.
4. I am certain that you will help me.
5. As I approached I heard a great noise.
6. He met me when I arrived.
7. The man admitted that he was wrong.
8. The girl was absent because she was ill.
9. You cannot succeed unless you work hard.
10. The witness described where the accident took place.

Replace the words underlined by a single word:

1. He wished to see him at once.
2. The concert was put off for a month.
3. The sentry ran away from his post.
4. The concert is held once every year.
5. The army went forward towards the town.
6. The man was sorry for his hasty words.
7. The sun went out of sight behind the clouds.
8. The people who live next door are very kind.
9. They made up their minds to go to the party.
10. That boy is always in time.

103

SENTENCES

SIMPLE TO COMPLEX

Make each pair of simple sentences into one complex sentence and retain the meaning as far as possible.

(Do not use **"and"** or **"but"** or **"so"**.)

1. *(a)* I have a dog.   *(b)* I am very fond of it.
2. *(a)* That is the man.   *(b)* He stole my purse.
3. *(a)* I was travelling in a bus.   *(b)* It collided with a taxi.
4. *(a)* The boy did not pass.   *(b)* His work was badly done.
5. *(a)* I was gazing out of the window   *(b)* I saw a crowd.
6. *(a)* The boy was riding a horse.   *(b)* It looked tired.
7. *(a)* The man could hardly walk.   *(b)* He carried such a heavy load.
8. *(a)* The book belongs to Jack.   *(b)* It is a red one.
9. *(a)* The girl went for the doctor.   *(b)* The doctor stayed next door.
10. *(a)* The house was destroyed.   *(b)* It was built by Tom's father.
11. *(a)* He works hard at his lessons.   *(b)* He wishes to succeed.
12. *(a)* The men were walking quickly.   *(b)* The men saw me.
13. *(a)* He heard the strains of music.   *(b)* He was passing a church.
14. *(a)* The lady lost the book.   *(b)* She was going to the library.
15. *(a)* The man stood at the door.   *(b)* The door was open.
16. *(a)* The boy caught a rabbit.   *(b)* He took it home.
17. *(a)* The girl fell heavily.   *(b)* The girl hurt herself.
18. *(a)* He opened the cupboard.   *(b)* He saw many books.
19. *(a)* The lady was careless.   *(b)* She lost her purse.
20. *(a)* Mary entered the room.   *(b)* The room was brightly decorated.
21. *(a)* A loud peal of thunder came.   *(b)* The children were frightened.
22. *(a)* Tom made mistakes in reading.   *(b)* He could not see well.
23. *(a)* The teacher praised the boys.   *(b)* They had worked well.
24. *(a)* The horse fell.   *(b)* It was pulling a heavy load.
25. *(a)* The man caught a salmon.   *(b)* He took it home.

26. *(a)* The boy has hurt his foot.   *(b)* The boy cannot walk.
27. *(a)* The lady sat in a coach.   *(b)* Four horses drew it.
28. *(a)* The tourist climbed the hill.   *(b)* The hill was steep.
29. *(a)* My sister has a good voice.   *(b)* She sings in the choir.
30. *(a)* The girl found a brooch.   *(b)* She took it to her mother.
31. *(a)* I found a lady's purse.   *(b)* It contained two coins.
32. *(a)* The girl wore a red dress.   *(b)* She sat next to me.
33. *(a)* I visited the little cottage.   *(b)* I was born in it.
34. *(a)* The woman was selling flowers.   *(b)* She stood at the corner of the street.
35. *(a)* I went to see my cousin.   *(b)* His home was in the country.
36. *(a)* The man was poorly clad.   *(b)* I gave him money.

COMPLEX TO SIMPLE

Change the following complex sentences into simple sentences and retain the meaning as far as possible:

1. He is a man who is very intelligent.
2. We heard the news that he was saved.
3. I can tell you how old he is.
4. The woman lives in a house which is very big.
5. He spoke to the soldier who was wounded.
6. The boy lost his ticket because he was careless.
7. I shall speak to him when he arrives.
8. The child found a ring which was very valuable.
9. He asked me where I lived.
10. Can you tell me which way the wind is blowing?
11. I saw him when the clock struck five.
12. We all believed the story that the traveller told.
13. Huge telescopes are used by the men who study the stars.
14. As soon as the sun rose the soldiers resumed their march.
15. He asked for the book in which one finds the meanings of words.
16. I admit that I have made a mistake.

ALPHABETICAL ORDER

The Alphabet (twenty-six letters)

A B C D E F G H I J K L M
N O P Q R S T U V W X Y Z

Practically all books containing lists have the words arranged in the order of the letters of the alphabet:

1. By the **first** letters of the words.
2. When the first letters are the same, the words are arranged according to the **second** letters.
3. When the first two letters are the same, the words are arranged according to the **third** letters.
   And so on.

Examples:
1. **By the first letter:**
   anchor, bicycle, height, machine, physical, seized, vehicle, yacht.
2. **When the first letters are the same:**
   absence, accurate, aeroplane, ancient, attention, autumn, awkward.
3. **When the first two letters are the same:**
   thatch, their, thimble, though, through, thumb, thyself.

EXERCISES

1. Place the following words in alphabetical order:
   vegetable, official, judgment, colonel, extremely, necessary, language, immediately.

2. Re-arrange the following words in dictionary order:
   beginning, brooch, biscuit, business, byre, bough, balance, blossom.

3. Place the following words in alphabetical order:
   complaint, cocoa, correct, coffee, condition, coarse, collection, course.

4. Re-arrange the following words in dictionary order:
   dismissed, disguise, displayed, disaster, district, discovery, disobeyed, disease.

THE APOSTROPHE

The Possessive Case of a Noun is shown by a mark (') known as an apostrophe.

In **Singular** nouns it is shown by **'s**, e.g. Mary's bag, the animal's foot, Keats's poems, Burns's songs. *Exception.* It may however be shown by the **apostrophe only (')** to avoid awkward-sounding double or treble s endings, e.g. Moses' anger, Jesus' words, Aristophanes' comedies.

In the **Plural** it is shown in **two** ways:

(a) **By the apostrophe only (')** when the plural ends in **-s** or **-es**, e.g. the boys' books, the ladies' coats.

(b) **By the apostrophe and s ('s)** when the **plural does not end in s**, e.g. the children's toys, the men's hats.

Singular Possessive	Plural Possessive
the girl's dress	the girls' dresses
the lady's bag	the ladies' bags
the boy's pencil	the boys' pencils
a day's work	seven days' work
the man's pipe	the men's pipes
the woman's glove	the women's gloves
the child's clothes	the children's clothes

EXERCISES

Correct the following sentences by putting in the apostrophes:

1. The boys pencil lay on the floor.
2. The ladies coats were in the cloakroom.
3. My cousins hand was badly hurt.
4. The mens boots were covered with mud.
5. The childs doll fell into the pond.
6. I saw that the object was a womans glove.
7. The register lay on the teachers desk.
8. He looked very smart in page-boys uniform.
9. It took several hours hard work to repair the damage.
10. In the window was a special display of babies clothes.
11. The childrens books were left in my uncles house.
12. The maids dress was torn by a neighbours dog.
13. My fathers wallet was discovered in the thieves den.
14. A ducks egg is generally cheaper than a hens.
15. Mr. Smiths watch is five minutes slower than Mr. Browns.

THE APOSTROPHE AS AN ABBREVIATION

When the apostrophe is used to abbreviate words it is placed where the letters have been omitted, e.g.

all's	all is	o'clock	of the clock
can't	cannot	o'er	over
couldn't	could not	shan't	shall not
'cross	across	she'll	she will
didn't	did not	shouldn't	should not
doesn't	does not	that's	that is
don't	do not	there's	there is
hasn't	has not	they'll	they will
haven't	have not	we'll	we will
he'd	he would	we've	we have
he'll	he will	whate'er	whatever
he's	he is	where'er	wherever
I'll	I will	whosoe'er	whosoever
I'd	I would	who've	who have
I'm	I am	won't	will not
isn't	is not	wouldn't	would not
it's	it is	you'll	you will
I've	I have	you're	you are

EXERCISES

1. Insert the apostrophe where it should be:

   tis, neednt, youll, Halloween, souwester, Ive, twas, neer, oclock, dont.

2. Write the following sentence making use of the apostrophe as an abbreviation:

   We will probably arrive at seven of the clock if there is a convenient omnibus.

CAPITAL LETTERS

Capital letters are used:

1. To begin sentences.
2. To begin special names.
3. To begin direct speech.
4. To begin words in titles.
5. To begin lines of poetry.
6. To begin words of exclamation.
7. To begin words He, Him, His, if they refer to God or Christ.
8. To write word "I".

1. **Beginning Sentences.**

   One day a girl was playing on a busy street. Her ball rolled into the middle of the road and she ran after it. At that moment a motor-car came dashing round the corner. A passer-by saw the girl's danger and ran quickly to her aid. Fortunately he saved her from serious injury.

2. **Special Names.**

   Jean Miller and her brother David are expected to arrive by Concorde from New York on Tuesday, November 30th, St. Andrew's Day.

3. **Direct Speech.**

   A man said to his friends, "If you manage to solve the puzzle, send me the answer." His companions replied, "We will send you our solution before the end of the week."

4. **Titles.**

   The famous collection of Indian animal stories called *The Jungle Book* was written by Rudyard Kipling.

5. **Lines of Poetry.**

   I wandered lonely as a cloud
      That floats on high o'er vales and hills,
   When all at once I saw a crowd,
      A host of golden daffodils,
   Beside the lake, beneath the trees,
   Fluttering and dancing in the breeze.

6. **Exclamation.**

   "Oh!" shouted the boy, "I have hurt my finger." "Indeed!" exclaimed his father, "You are lucky to get off so lightly."

Capital Letters

7. **Reference to God or Christ.**
    After Jesus had preached to the multitude He proceeded on His way to Jerusalem.

8. **The Pronoun "I".**
    He advised me to travel by 'bus but I told him that I preferred to travel by rail.

PUNCTUATION

By correct punctuation we mean the proper use of:
capital letters, comma (,), period (.), quotation marks (" "), exclamation mark (!), question mark (?), and apostrophe (').

Punctuate the following sentences:

1. What time is it asked the traveller
2. His father said where is your brothers knife
3. My friend exclaimed what a lovely view
4. He has gone to school said his sister in a quiet voice
5. The child suddenly shouted look
6. Oh cried the boy i have hurt my finger
7. Come here said his mother all right replied the boy
8. The man asked have you seen the hammer yes replied his companion it is on the table
9. A boy said to his chum are you going to the pictures no replied the other im on my way home
10. When i return said the girl to her father will you tell me the story of the shipwreck very well he answered but dont be too long at your aunts

DIMINUTIVES

booklet	coronet	bannerette	dearie	chicken
bracelet	cygnet	briquette	girlie	kitten
goblet	eaglet	cigarette	laddie	maiden
leaflet	islet	epaulette	lassie	cubicle
ringlet	latchet	kitchenette	bullock	icicle
rivulet	leveret	pipette	hillock	particle
streamlet	locket	rosette	damsel	lambkin
baronet	owlet	statuette	morsel	mannikin
circlet	pocket	wagonette	satchel	napkin
codling	darling	duckling	gosling	porkling
sapling	seedling	nestling	globule	molecule

SMALL QUANTITIES

air	. a breath, puff, whiff	paper	. a scrap
bread	. a crumb, crust, morsel	rain	. a drop, spot
butter	. a pat, nut	salt	. a grain, pinch
colour	. a dab, tint, touch	sand	. a grain, particle
corn	. an ear	smoke	. a wisp
dirt	. a particle, speck, spot	snuff	. a pinch
energy	. an ounce	soot	. a smut, speck
flowers	. a nosegay, posy	straw	. a wisp
food	. a morsel, particle, scrap	sugar	. a grain, spoonful
glass	. a splinter, fragment	tea	. a pinch, spoonful
grass	. a blade, tuft	time	. a moment, second
hair	. a lock, strand	water	. a drop, sip
light	. a beam, glimmer, ray	wind	. a puff, whiff
liquid	. a drop, sip	wood	. a chip, splinter

FOR REFERENCE

	To Find	Look at
1.	the address of a person	directory
2.	the meaning of a word	dictionary
3.	the day and date of the month	calendar
4.	the position of a place	atlas
5.	a list of priced goods or books	catalogue
6.	a telephone number	telephone directory
7.	the time of a train or bus	time-table
8.	record of a ship's progress at sea	log
9.	record of attendance	register
10.	record of personal daily events	diary
11.	collection of photos and autographs	album
12.	extracts from books and papers	scrap-book
13.	record of recent happenings	newspaper
14.	facts regarding days of the year	almanac
15.	a fictitious tale	novel
16.	a life story	biography
17.	material regarding living creatures	book on zoology
18.	material regarding plants	book on botany
19.	material regarding the stars	book on astronomy
20.	material regarding the Earth's crust	book on geology

PROVERBS

Proverbs are popular sayings expressed in a clever, brief manner.

1. A bad workman quarrels with his tools.
2. Absence makes the heart grow fonder.
3. A bird in the hand is worth two in the bush.
4. A cat may look at a king.
5. A drowning man will clutch at a straw.
6. A fool and his money are soon parted.
7. A friend in need is a friend indeed.
8. A hungry man is an angry man.
9. All's well that ends well.
10. An apple a day keeps the doctor away.
11. Any time means no time.
12. A miss is as good as a mile.
13. A penny saved is a penny gained.
14. A rolling stone gathers no moss.
15. A stitch in time saves nine.
16. As well be hanged for a sheep as a lamb.
17. A small leak will sink a great ship.
18. As the twig is bent so the tree's inclined.
19. As you make your bed so must you lie in it.
20. A wild goose never laid a tame egg.
21. Better half a loaf than no bread.
22. Better late than never.
23. Birds of a feather flock together.
24. Charity begins at home.
25. Cut your coat according to your cloth.
26. Discretion is the better part of valour.
27. Don't carry all your eggs in one basket.
28. Don't count your chickens before they are hatched.
29. Early to bed — early to rise, etc.
30. Empty vessels make most sound.
31. Enough is as good as a feast.
32. Every cloud has a silver lining.
33. Every dog has its day.
34. Example is better than precept.
35. Exchange is no robbery.
36. Experience teacheth fools.
37. Faint heart never won fair lady.
38. Fine feathers make fine birds.

112

39. Fine words butter no parsnips.
40. Fire is a good servant but a bad master.
41. First come, first served.
42. Forbidden fruit tastes sweetest.
43. Good wine needs no bush.
44. Grasp all, lose all.
45. Great minds think alike.
46. Great oaks from little acorns grow.
47. Habit is second nature.
48. Half a loaf is better than none.
49. He laughs best who laughs last.
50. He pays the piper who calls the tune.
51. He goes a-sorrowing who goes a-borrowing.
52. Hunger is the best sauce.
53. Imitation is the sincerest form of flattery.
54. In for a penny, in for a pound.
55. It's a long lane that has no turning.
56. It's an ill wind that blows nobody any good.
57. Laugh and grow fat.
58. Leave well alone.
59. Let not the pot call the kettle black.
60. Let sleeping dogs lie.
61. Listeners hear no good of themselves.
62. Little boys should be seen and not heard.
63. Little pitchers have long ears.
64. Look after the pence, and the pounds will look after themselves.
65. Look before you leap.
66. Love laughs at locksmiths.
67. Make hay while the sun shines.
68. Misery makes strange bedfellows.
69. More haste, less speed.
70. Necessity is the mother of invention.
71. New brooms sweep clean.
72. None but the brave deserve the fair.
73. None so deaf as those who will not hear.
74. No news is good news.
75. No smoke without fire.
76 Once bitten twice shy.
77. One good turn deserves another.
78. One man's meat is another man's poison.

Proverbs

79. One swallow does not make a summer.
80. Out of sight, out of mind.
81. Out of the frying pan into the fire.
82. Penny wise, pound foolish.
83. Pride goeth before a fall.
84. Robbing Peter to pay Paul.
85. Sauce for the goose is sauce for the gander.
86. Set a thief to catch a thief.
87. Shoemakers' wives are worst shod.
88. Silence gives consent.
89. Spare the rod and spoil the child.
90. Speech is silvern, silence is golden.
91. Still waters run deep.
92. The least said the soonest mended.
93. The early bird catches the worm.
94. Too many cooks spoil the broth.
95. Truth will out.
96. Two heads are better than one.
97. Union is strength.
98. We never miss the water till the well runs dry.
99. Where there's a will there's a way.
100. When the cat's away the mice will play.

COLLOQUIALISMS

Colloquialisms are expressions used in common conversation.

The apple of one's eye	somebody specially dear.
Armed to the teeth	completely armed.
A wet blanket	a discouraging person.
Dead beat	exhausted.
In the same boat	in same circumstances.
Carried away	highly excited.
A chip of the old block	very like father.
Off his chump	off his head, mad.
Under a cloud	in trouble or disfavour.
Down in the mouth	in low spirits.
Down on one's luck	in ill-luck.
All ears	paying close attention.
At a loose end	having nothing to do.
A queer fish	an odd person.
Off form	not so capable as usual.
Good for nothing	useless.
A son of a gun	a likeable rogue.
Hard of hearing	almost deaf.
Hard up	short of money.
Hard hit	seriously troubled.
In evil case	poor.
Ill-used	badly treated.
Lion-hearted	of great courage.
At loggerheads	quarrelling.
The man in the street	an ordinary man.
Up to the mark	good enough, well enough.
An old salt	an experienced sailor.
A peppery individual	a cranky, hot-tempered person.
A pocket Hercules	small but strong.
At rest	dead.
A rough diamond	a person of real worth but rough manners.
Silver-tongued	plausible and eloquent.
Golden-voiced	pleasing to hear.
Purse-proud	conceited about money.
Out of sorts	not well.
On the level	honest.
Stuck up	conceited.
Thick in the head	stupid.
Beside oneself	out of one's mind (with anger, grief).
Heavy-eyed	sleepy.

GENERAL COLLOQUIAL EXPRESSIONS

To	To
weigh anchor	lift the anchor.
keep up appearances	maintain an outward show.
have a bee in one's bonnet	be obsessed with an idea.
put one's best foot forward	do best possible.
sweep the board	take all.
make no bones about it	be plain and outspoken.
burn the candle at both ends	overdo work and play.
have one's heart in one's boots	be very despondent.
have one's heart in one's mouth	be frightened.
bury the hatchet	make peace.
discover a mare's nest	pretend a discovery in order to hoax.
draw the long bow	tell incredible stories.
make a clean breast of	confess.
have a feather in one's cap	have something to be proud of.
set one's cap at	try to captivate.
throw up the sponge	give up the struggle.
throw in the cards	give up the struggle.
throw in the towel	give up the struggle.
cast up	reproach.
show a clean pair of heels	escape by running.
pull up short	stop suddenly.
wait till the clouds roll by	await more favourable circumstances.
turn one's coat	change one's principles or allegiance.
pay a man in his own coin	give tit for tat.
give the cold shoulder	show indifference or ignore.
throw cold water on	discourage.
have a crow to pluck with	have something to settle.
cut a dash	be very showy.
lead a dance	delude.
lead up the garden	deceive by hiding real intention.
keep a thing dark	hide something.
keep one's distance	stay aloof.
lead a dog's life	have a wretched life.
draw the line	fix the limit.
keep one's powder dry	be ready or prepared.
throw dust in the eyes	deceive.
make both ends meet	manage financially.
face the music	meet the worst.
sit on the fence	avoid taking sides.

116

General Colloquial Expressions

To	To
put one's foot in it	cause embarrassment by word or action.
fall foul of	come up against.
get into hot water	get into trouble.
take French leave	go without permission.
play the game	act fairly.
hit below the belt	act unfairly.
hold one's tongue	keep silent.
blow one's trumpet	boast.
hit the nail on the head	be right.
kick up a dust	create a row.
bite the dust	fall to the ground, be defeated.
kick over the traces	throw off control.
knock on the head	stop suddenly.
turn over a new leaf	conduct oneself better.
pull one's leg	hoax.
tell it to the Marines	no-one believes that.
go through the mill	undergo suffering.
put the cart before the horse	start at the wrong end.
make the mouth water	cause to desire.
sling mud	slander.
nip in the bud	stop at an early stage.
send one packing	dismiss quickly.
pad the hoof	walk.
play fast and loose	act carelessly.
keep the pot boiling	keep an activity going.
rain cats and dogs	rain very heavily.
raise one's dander	anger.
mind your p's and q's	be careful about your behaviour.
raise the wind	obtain money.
smell a rat	be suspicious.
take a rise out of	fool.
rub the wrong way	irritate by opposing.
get into hot water	get into trouble.
turn the tables	reverse a result.
back chat	give impudence.
ride the high horse	be snobbish, arrogant.
let the cat out of the bag	tell what should be kept secret.
send to Coventry	ignore as a punishment.
haul over the coals	scold or punish.

General Colloquial Expressions

To	To
take the bull by the horns	act despite risks.
strike while the iron is hot	act without delay.
take forty winks	sleep.
chew the fat	argue.
act the goat	behave foolishly.
live from hand to mouth	live in hardship.
hang one's head	feel ashamed.
turn up one's nose	scorn deliberately.
play with fire	tempt serious trouble.
swing the lead	avoid work purposely.
blaze the trail	lead the way.
come a cropper	fail or to fall to earth.
go on all fours	travel on hands and knees OR entreat most humbly.

POPULAR PHRASES

Explain what is meant by the following phrases:

horse play	back to the wall
for a lark	from pillar to post
a fine kettle of fish	a bird's eye view
as the crow flies	a busman's holiday
a stiff upper lip	no flies on him
a blind alley	not worth the candle
a hen on a hot girdle	a dead cert
a cat on hot bricks	a cock and bull story
a far cry	with flying colours
a flash in the pan	a fly in the ointment
every man Jack	the lion's share
on the nail	not a patch on
pins and needles	bats in the belfry
a storm in a teacup	by hook or by crook

DOUBLES — Used in Speech to give greater emphasis

1. **By repetition of actual word:**
   again and again, by and by, neck and neck, out and out, over and over, round and round, so and so, such and such.

2. **By repetition of meaning:**
   beck and call, ways and means, far and away, puff and blow, null and void, stuff and nonsense, fast and furious, odds and ends, rant and rave, lean and lanky, out and away, hue and cry, bawl and shout, old and grey.

3. **By alliteration (words beginning with the same letter):**
   humming and hawing, kith and kin, might and main, part and parcel, safe and sound, hale and hearty, spick and span, alas and alack, time and tide, rack and ruin, rough and ready, one and only.

4. **By opposites:**
   this and that, thick and thin, on and off, great and small, in and out, high and low, come and go, give and take, one and all, ups and downs, here and there.

5. **By words of similar sound:**
   high and dry, fair and square, out and about, wear and tear.

6. **By related words:**
   heart and soul, hip and thigh, tooth and nail, body and soul, root and branch, lock and key, hammer and tongs, hole and corner, head and shoulders, hand and foot.

7. **Other examples:**
   all and sundry, fast and loose, fits and starts, hard and fast, free and easy, rough and tumble, habit and repute, over and above, touch and go, time and again.

EXERCISES

Place the following phrases in the most suitable sentences:

again and again, lock and key, spick and span, puff and blow, odds and ends.

1. The police placed the man under ....
2. He polished his boots until they were ....
3. She tried to do it ....
4. The child had gathered many ....
5. The stout man began to .... with exertion.

COLOURS

The following are the colours of the rainbow:

violet, indigo, blue, green, yellow, orange, red.

There are other colours, such as:

white, black, purple, brown, pink, grey, crimson.

Sometimes we refer to things as being:

blood-red, bottle-green, brick-red, cinnamon-brown, coal-black, milk-white, nut-brown, pea-green, primrose-yellow, rose-pink, ruby-red, russet-brown, sea-green, shell-pink, sky-blue, slate-grey, snow-white.

Often we make use of **"colour"** words in everyday speech, e.g.:

1. I saw it in **black and white**.
   I saw it in writing (or print).

2. I am in his **black books**.
   He is displeased with me.

3. The man was a **blackguard**.
   The man was a low scoundrel.

4. He was the **black sheep** of the family.
   He disgraced his family.

5. The man **looked blue**.
   The man looked as if he was depressed in spirits.

6. He was in a **blue funk**.
   He was in great terror.

7. He had **blue blood** in his veins.
   He was of aristocratic descent.

8. His brother was a **bluejacket**.
   His brother was a seaman in the navy.

9. The **green-eyed monster** caused him to strike his friend.
   Jealousy caused him to strike his friend.

10. He was a **greenhorn** at the game.
    He was raw and inexperienced at the game.

11. "Do you see any **green in my eye**?"
    "Do I look as if I could be easily imposed upon?"

120

12. The fellow was **yellow at heart**.
    The fellow was really a coward.

13. He was born **in the purple**.
    He was of royal birth.

14. The man showed the **white feather**.
    The man showed signs of cowardice.

15. The business was a **white elephant**.
    The business was a failure.

16. It was a **red letter day** for me.
    It was a notable and fortunate day for me.

EXERCISES

Complete the following sentences:

The old colonel was purple with ....
The bully turned white with ....
The little orphan was blue with ....
His rival was green with ....
The pages of the book were yellow with ....

OUR FIVE SENSES

Every normal person is born with five senses by which he or she is able to see, hear, smell, taste and touch.

Sight — is the ability to observe or perceive by the <u>eye</u>.

Hearing — is the ability to listen or perceive by the <u>ear</u>.

Smell — is the ability to detect odour or perceive by the <u>nose</u>.

Taste — is the ability to detect flavour in the mouth or perceive by the <u>tongue</u>.

Touch — is the ability to detect objects by contact or perceive by <u>feeling</u>.

DERIVATIONS

A **Root** is a word in its first and simplest form. A word may be built up or have its meaning changed by an addition at either end. The addition at the beginning is known as a **Prefix**, e.g. dis-agree. The addition at the end is known as a **Suffix**, e.g. paint-er.

ROOTS

Word	Meaning	Examples
aqua	water	aquatic, aqueduct
audio	I hear	audible, audience, audit
capio	I take	capable, captive, capture
centum	a hundred	centenarian, century
clamo	I shout	clamour, proclaim, exclaim
creo	create	creation, creature
curro	I run	courier, current, excursion
decem	ten	December, decimal
dico	I say	edict, dictation, verdict, dictator
duco	I lead	produce, reduce, introduce
facio	I make	fact, factory, perfect
finis	an end	final, infinite
fortis	strong	fort, fortify
homo	a man	homicide, human
impero	I command	empire, emperor, imperial
liber	free	liberal, liberty
malus	bad	malady, malice, maltreat
manus	hand	manual, manufacture, manuscript
mitto	I send	missile, mission, remittance
navis	a ship	navigate, navy
octo	eight	octagon, octave, October
pello	I drive	expel, propel, repel
pendeo	I hang	depend, pendant, suspend
pes	a foot	pedal, pedestrian, quadruped
planus	level	plain, plan, plane
plus	more	plural, surplus
porto	I carry	export, import, porter, transport
poto	I drink	poison, potion
primus	first	primer, primitive, Prime Minister
rego	I rule	regal, regent, regiment
rota	a wheel	rotate, rote, rotund
ruptus	broken	eruption, interruption, rupture

Derivations

Word	Meaning	Examples
scribo	I write	scripture, describe, manuscript
specio	I see	aspect, prospect, spectacles
teneo	I hold	contain, retain, tentacles
unus	one	unit, unity, union
vanus	empty	vanish, vanity, vain
venio	I come	adventure, prevent, venture
video	I see	provident, visible, vision
vinco	I overcome	convince, victory
voco	I call	revoke, vocal, voice
volvo	I roll	evolve, revolve, volume

PREFIXES

Prefix	Meaning	Examples
a	on	afloat, ashore, aloft
a-, ab-, abs-	away, from	avert, absolve, abstract
ad-, ac-, ar- (etc.)	to	adhere, accept, arrive, assume, attract
ante-	before	antecedent, anteroom
anti-	against	antagonist, anti-aircraft
bi-, bis-	two, twice	bicycle, biped, bisect, biscuit
circum-	round	circumference, circuit
com-, con-	together	comparison, competition, contact
contra-	against	contrary, contraband, contradiction
de-	down	depress, descend, describe
dif-, dis-	apart, not	different, disagree, disappear
ex-	out of	exhale, export, extract
fore-	before	forecast, forenoon, foretell, foresee
im-, in-	in, into	import, include
in-	not	incapable, inhuman
inter-	between	international, interrupt, interval
mis-	wrong	misdeed, misjudge, mistake
ob-	against	object, obstruction
post-	after	postpone, postscript, post-war
pre-	before	predict, prepare, pre-war
pro-	forth	proceed, produce
re-	back	retake, return, retrace
sub-	under	submarine, subway
trans-	across	transfer, transport, transpose
un-	not, without	unfit, unknown, unpaid, unsafe
vice-	instead	vice-captain, viceroy

Derivations

SUFFIXES

Suffix	Meaning	Examples
-able, -ible	capable of being	movable, eatable, incredible
-ain, -an	one connected	chaplain, publican
-ance, -ence	state of	repentance, existence
-ant	one who	assistant, servant
-el, -et, -ette	little	satchel, locket, cigarette
-er, -eer, -ier	one who	baker, engineer, furrier
-ess	the female	goddess, princess, waitress
-fy	to make	glorify, purify, simplify
-icle, -sel	little	particle, morsel
-less	without	careless, guiltless, merciless
-ling	little	codling, gosling, darling
-ment	state of being	merriment, enjoyment
-ock	little	hillock, bittock
-oon, -on	large	saloon, balloon, flagon
-ory	a place for	dormitory, factory
-ous	full of	famous, glorious, momentous

EXERCISES

1. Underline **the root parts** of the following words and give their meanings:

   century, December, factory, manual, navigate, suspend, pedal, export, describe, tentacles.

2. Underline **the prefixes** in the following words and give their meanings:

   anteroom, bicycle, circumference, contradict, forenoon, international, postscript, submarine, transport, unknown.

3. Underline **the suffixes** in the following words and give their meanings:

   heiress, cigarette, explorer, simplify, duckling, careless, edible, attendant, decorator, courageous.

In the following list many questions can be answered by one word. Wherever possible, do so.

1. A boy who frightens weaker boys.
2. A number of soldiers.
3. The men who work on a ship.
4. Children in a school.
5. A man who protects sheep.
6. The low ground between two hills.
7. A place where pupils are educated.
8. A ship which travels below the surface of the sea.
9. A place for storing a motor car.
10. A small leaf.
11. The woman in charge of nurses.
12. A field in which fruit trees grow.
13. An instrument for measuring time.
14. From what do we make butter?
15. A man who makes furniture.
16. A fertile place in the desert.
17. A man who pretends to be good.
18. A person who is always boasting.
19. A stream which flows into a river.
20. A hundred years.
21. Name instrument for telling direction.
22. What are the steps of a ladder called?
23. Name two spotted animals.
24. A doctor who performs operations.
25. What is the front part of a ship called?
26. Headgear worn by some inhabitants of India.
27. A place where beer is made.
28. What is daybreak sometimes termed?
29. A man who draws and paints.
30. Fish with the bones taken out.
31. A shallow crossing in a river.
32. Two creatures which see well in the dark.
33. What is the meaning of plume?
34. Name any American money.
35. Girl or woman who serves at table.
36. A person who by desire lives alone.
37. What do we call the breaking of a bone?

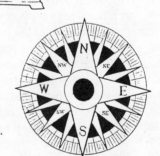

General Knowledge

38. Name two shellfish.
39. What is the flesh of a sheep called?
40. The first meal of the day.
41. Quick ways of sending messages.
42. Name of metal container for oil.
43. Place in which photographs are taken.
44. A place where people are buried.
45. Another name for a policeman.
46. Name three "string" instruments.
47. Name imaginary line round middle of earth.
48. An instrument which measures heat and cold.
49. From what do we make cheese?
50. Name the five human senses.

51. What kind of fish is a kipper?
52. Type of footwear in hot countries.
53. A place where whisky is made.
54. Another name for a street sweeper.
55. Name three infectious diseases.
56. What lights must a steamer show at night?
57. Name two striped animals.
58. Goods carried out of a country.
59. A place where birds are kept.
60. Person who gives life in a good cause.
61. The air surrounding the earth.
62. A person who saves and hoards money.
63. A religious song.
64. How does a fish breathe in water?
65. Name the colours of the rainbow.
66. What is the small top room of a house?
67. Which is Britain's fiercest wild bird?
68. What is the national dress of Scotland?
69. A three-sided figure.
70. A place where aeroplanes are kept.
71. Meaning of "The Seven Seas".
72. A vessel for holding flowers.
73. What is the meaning of steed?
74. Name patron saint of England.
75. A person who cannot hear or speak.
76. A room on board a ship.
77. A soldier with three stripes on each arm.

78. A person who takes the place of another.
79. How many legs has a fly?
80. Name four kinds of tree.
81. A place where iron goods are made.
82. Name four great deserts.
83. Name three animals living mostly in water.
84. A man who does tricks with cards.
85. Water which has turned into gas.

86. What birds are common to our city streets?
87. What is the flesh of a pig called?
88. Scottish loch in which there is said to be a monster.
89. Goods taken into a country.
90. A place where leather is made.
91. Another name for a donkey.
92. Machine which makes electricity.
93. What is milk-fat called?
94. What is wind?
95. Who is a Jack Tar?
96. What is a tripod?
97. Who is a colleen?
98. What is the flesh of the deer called?
99. Name for smuggled goods.

100. What is a pigmy?
101. A place where chickens are hatched.
102. What is an astronaut?
103. What are the primary colours?
104. Of what wood is a cricket bat made?
105. Give motto of The Boys' Brigade.
106. What is the Milky Way?
107. Name the tin for holding tea.
108. Place where gas is stored.

109. What is the Crow's Nest to a sailor?
110. Explain lbw.
111. What is a boneshaker?
112. Which is the lightest common metal?
113. Explain meaning of a dead language.
114. Where is the longest wall in the world?
115. What is a cow-catcher?
116. A place where fish are kept.
117. Who was Man Friday?

General Knowledge

118. What is a mimic?
119. Where is the playground of Europe?
120. Give common name for the spine.
121. What is a planet?
122. What is meant by scuttling a ship?
123. Give motto of the Boy Scouts.
124. In which country do people wear wooden shoes?
125. What is a grotto?
126. Name three "wind" instruments.
127. A place where you can lunch for payment.
128. A black man.
129. A white man.
130. What is the basin of a river?
131. What is capital punishment?
132. What is the "Herring Pond"?
133. Who was Long John Silver?
134. What is a tailor's goose?
135. What side is starboard?
136. Who is the patron saint of Scotland?

137. What is meant by "crossing the line"?
138. What is a fleece of wool?
139. Who is our present Prime Minister?
140. Which month contains the longest day?
141. Which country is called Erin?
142. Name two "percussion" instruments.
143. What is a song for two called?
144. Name an oil used as a medicine.
145. How many in a "Baker's dozen"?
146. What is a centenarian?
147. Instrument used for drawing circles.
148. What is a bandbox?
149. What cap badge do postmen wear?
150. What is the "Key of the Mediterranean"?
151. Which insect makes honey?
152. Name any animal covered with spines.

153. When is signal "S.O.S" used?
154. When is Christmas Day?
155. What is a claymore?
156. Where is John o' Groats?
157. How many teeth has an adult person?

158. Who is the patron saint of Ireland?
159. What do we call water when solid?
160. What is a dirk?
161. Name any "pouched" animals.
162. What is a fishplate?
163. An instrument for seeing tiny objects.
164. Who was David Livingstone?
165. Which month contains the shortest day?
166. What is Lochnagar?
167. Name five common garden flowers.
168. Which country is called Albyn?
169. What is a storey?
170. Which animal is called the "King of Beasts"?

171. Who is the patron saint of Wales?
172. A funny drawing of general interest.
173. What is Benbecula?
174. Another name for an airman.
175. What is a burnous?
176. What is a bed on board a ship called?
177. What kind of person is a dude?
178. Give distance between tram or railway lines.
179. What is a gamp?
180. Which animal covers great distances without water?
181. What is a hobo?
182. Name any plants associated with your country.
183. What is a rickshaw?
184. Name gas which supports life and flame.
185. A number of icebergs.
186. City famous for high buildings.
187. Another name for an aeroplane.
188. What is a weather satellite?
189. Name insect which carries malaria fever.
190. What is the yellow part of an egg called?
191. Who was Mars?
192. When is a person said to be myopic?
193. Name given to a sailor's map.
194. What is the skin of the orange called?
195. Name given to a barrel cork.
196. Another word meaning remedy.
197. Soldiers on horseback.

General Knowledge

198. What is meant by a bird's-eye view?
199. Who is a sheik?
200. What is used for making tea?
201. What is a bloater?
202. How is bronze made?
203. Another name for a learner.
204. What is the Aurora Borealis?
205. American dog used to pull sledges.
206. Stone bowl used to make flour.
207. What is a thermos flask?
208. Way out sign above door.
209. Who is a clergyman?
210. The top of a hill or mountain.
211. What is coral?
212. Meaning of umpire.
213. Name of rope used by cowboy?
214. What is meant by walking in Indian file?
215. To what country does a "Yankee" belong?
216. Another name for a village.

217. What is a banshee?
218. Name given to soldiers on foot.
219. A place from which stone or slate is obtained.
220. A pocket case for holding money and documents.
221. Another name for an inn.
222. What is the white of an egg called?
223. Give another word meaning salary.
224. What is meant by walking abreast?
225. What is a coyote?
226. What is peculiar about a Manx cat?
227. From what do we obtain coffee?
228. What is a cog wheel?
229. Name an animal which chews the cud.
230. What is a cataract?
231. Which letters are vowels?
232. Name any beast of prey.
233. Why was Peter Pan different from other children?
234. What is a Lunar Probe?
235. What is a life-buoy?
236. From what tree would you expect acorns to fall?
237. Which animal has a tail called a brush?

238. What is a gondola?
239. From what do we obtain cider?
240. What is a carnivorous creature?
241. Name stuff used to treat stings.
242. What is meant by "The Sign of the Three Brass Balls"?
243. What is the hand-rail for a stair called?
244. What is a nuclear power station?
245. A clergyman's house is called a ....
246. What is meant by "The Dark Continent"?
247. Name stuff used to treat burns.
248. Where is the "New World"?
249. Name an animal with a very long neck.
250. What is veal?
251. Name stuff used to treat cuts.
252. What is the little white tail of the rabbit called?
253. Name an insect which appears to carry a lamp.
254. What is a nightmare?
255. Which creatures have antlers?
256. What is a hod?
257. Which bird appears to have a white waistcoat?
258. Name given to a young tree.
259. What is the middle part of an apple called?

FASTENINGS

Name things fastened by the following:

bar and hasp	cord	latch	rope
belt	fishplate	lock	solder
bolt	glue	mortar	staple
braces	gum	nail	strap and buckle
brooch	handcuffs	padlock	string
button	harness	paste	strut
cable	hawsers	peg	tack
cement	hinge	pin	thread
chain	hook and eye	putty	twine
clip	lace	rivet	zip

131

USEFUL INFORMATION

The Races of Mankind differ in a number of inherited features, e.g. skin colour; shape of nose, eyes, lips; type and colour of hair. They are:

Mongolian. *"Yellow"*. *Most numerous*. Yellow, copper skin; fairly broad nose, low bridge; slanting eyes; black coarse hair. Chinese, Japanese, Siberian and South-East Asians, Eskimos, American Indians, Laplanders.

Caucasian. *"Whites"*. Pink, olive, light brown skin; high narrow nose; eyes light, more recessed; hair fair, wavy or straight, more beard. Europeans and their American descendants, South-West Asians, Indians, other South Asians and some Pacific islanders.

Negro. *"Blacks"*. Black or dark brown skin; broad nose, thick lips; black, brown woolly hair, less beard. African peoples and American descendants, Papuans and some other Pacific islanders.

The **Principal Languages of the World** are as follows (arranged according to the number speaking each): Chinese, English, Russian, Western Hindi, Spanish, German, French, Japanese, Portuguese and Italian.

The **Continents** are: Europe, Asia, Africa, America and Australia.

The **Oceans** are: Atlantic, Pacific, Indian, Arctic and Antarctic.

The **Largest Islands** (other than the continents) are: Greenland, New Guinea, Borneo, Madagascar and Baffin Land.

The **Greatest Lakes** are: Caspian Sea (U.S.S.R.), Lake Superior (North America), Victoria Nyanza (Central Africa), Aral Sea (U.S.S.R.), Lake Huron (North America) and Lake Michigan (North America).

The **Highest Mountains of the World** are all in the Himalayan Mountain Range in Northern India. They are: Mt. Everest, Mt. Godwin-Austin, Mt. Kangchenjunga, Mt. Nanga Parbat and Mt. Kamet.

The **Longest Rivers** are: Missouri-Mississippi (United States), Amazon (Brazil), Nile (Egypt), Yangtse (China), Lena (U.S.S.R), Zaire (Central Africa), Niger (West Africa) and Yenesei (U.S.S.R.).

The **Largest Cities of the World** are: London (England), New York (U.S.A.), Tokyo (Japan), Berlin (Germany), Chicago (U.S.A.), Shanghai (China), Paris (France) and Moscow (U.S.S.R.).

VARIOUS COUNTRIES — THE PEOPLES — THEIR LANGUAGE

Country	People	Language
Australia	Australians	English
Belgium	Belgians	Flemish, French
Bulgaria	Bulgarians	Bulgarian
Canada	Canadians	English, French
Chinese People's Republic	Chinese	Chinese
Czechoslovakia	Czechs, Slovaks	Czech
Denmark	Danes	Danish
Egypt	Egyptians	Arabic
England	English	English
Finland	Finns	Finnish
France	French	French
Germany	Germans	German
Greece	Greeks	Greek
Holland	Dutch	Dutch
Hungary	Hungarians	Magyar
India	Indians	Hindustani
Iran	Iranians	Persian
Ireland (Eire)	Irish	English, Gaelic
Israel	Jews, Arabs	Hebrew, Arabic
Italy	Italians	Italian
Japan	Japanese	Japanese
Kenya	Kenyan	Swahili, English
Mexico	Mexicans	Spanish
New Zealand	{ New Zealanders	English
	Maoris	Maori
Nigeria	Nigerians	Yoruba, Hausa, Ibo
Poland	Poles	Polish
Portugal	Portuguese	Portuguese
Saudi Arabia	Arabs	Arabic
Scotland	Scots	English, Gaelic
South Africa	South Africans	English, Afrikaans
Spain	Spaniards	Spanish
Switzerland	Swiss	French, German, Italian
Turkey	Turks	Turkish
United States	Americans	English
* U.S.S.R.	Russians	Russian
Wales	Welsh	English, Cymric

* The people of the Soviet Union are commonly called the "Russians", but this vast country comprises many peoples other than true Russians, speaking many languages other than Russian.

Useful Information

ORIGIN OF CERTAIN PLACE NAMES

Asia, the largest continent, takes its name from the district behind Smyrna in Turkey. We sometimes refer to the eastern part of the continent as the "Orient" (Land of the Rising Sun).

America is named after Amerigo Vespucci, who explored parts of the coastline of the New World, shortly after its discovery by Columbus.

Europe — Some say it was named Eref by the Phoenicians, meaning "The Land of the Setting Sun" and sometimes referred to as the "Occident". Others say it was named after Europus, a town in Macedonia.

Africa was so named by the Romans after the Afri tribe of Tunisia.

Australia means the "Southern Continent".

Nigeria — Nigeria was named after the River Niger.

Australia — see above.
National Emblems — Kangaroo, Emu, Mimosa.

Canada — from American Indian word "Kannata", meaning "a number of settlers' huts".
National Emblems — Maple Leaf, Beaver.

China (The Chinese people seldom use this name but generally refer to the Province concerned). The word is said to have come from "Tsin", the ruler who built the Great Wall of China.
National Emblems — Dragon, Plum Blossom.

England — land of the Angles, who invaded and conquered South Britain in the 5th century.
National Emblems — Lion, Rose, Bulldog.

France — (Old name Gaul — land of the Gauls). Present name from the Franks, who later conquered the country.
National Emblems — Lily, Cock, Eagle.

Germany — "Germanus" (neighbour), a Roman word borrowed from the Gauls. Germans call their country "Deutschland".
National Emblems — Eagle, Corn Flower.

India — the land through which the River Indus has its course.
National Emblems — Elephant, Star, Lotus, Jasmine.

Ireland (Gaelic name — Eire) — land of the Irish tribe.
National Emblems — Shamrock, Harp.

Italy (= vitalia) — means "cattle or pasture land".
National Emblems — Eagle, Lily, Laurel wreath.

Japan — The Japanese always use the word "Nippon" and both mean "The Land of the Rising Sun".
National Emblems — Chrysanthemum, Rising Sun.

New Zealand — (New Sea Land) — so named by a Dutch explorer after Zealand — a part of Holland.
National Emblems — Kiwi, Fern.

Russia — land of the tribe of Russ.
National Emblems — Hammer and Sickle, Five-pointed Star.

Scotland — (Old name Caledonia). Present name from the Scots, a north of Ireland tribe, who invaded and gradually became masters of the whole country.
National Emblems — Lion, Thistle.

South Africa — (see "Africa").
National Emblems — Springbok, Wagon.

Spain — English form of the word "Hispania" or "Espana". The name comes from "Shapan" (rabbit land), as the Phoenicians found the country over-run with these animals.
National Emblems — Red Carnation, Pomegranate.

U.S.A. — (see "America").
National Emblems — Eagle, Buffalo, Golden Rod.

Turkey — land of the Turks.
National Emblem — Star and Crescent.

Wales — (Old name Cymru — land of the Cymry tribe). Present name is derived from Anglo-Saxon word meaning "land of the foreigner".
National Emblems — Leek, Daffodil, Dragon.

Useful Information

VARIOUS COUNTRIES AND THEIR CAPITALS

Country	Capital	Country	Capital
Albania	Tirana	Italy	Rome
Argentine	Buenos Aires	Japan	Tokyo
Australia	Canberra	Kenya	Nairobi
Belgium	Brussels	New Zealand	Wellington
Brazil	Brasilia	Nigeria	Lagos
Bulgaria	Sofia	Norway	Oslo
Canada	Ottawa	Pakistan	Islamabad
Chinese People's		Poland	Warsaw
Republic	Beijing, Peking	Portugal	Lisbon
Czechoslovakia	Prague	Rumania	Bucharest
Denmark	Copenhagen	Scotland	Edinburgh
Egypt	Cairo	Spain	Madrid
Eire	Dublin	Sri Lanka	Colombo
England	London	Sweden	Stockholm
France	Paris	Switzerland	Berne
Germany (West)	Bonn	Turkey	Ankara
Germany (East)	East Berlin	Republic of	
Greece	Athens	South Africa	Cape Town
Holland	Amsterdam	United States	Washington
Hungary	Budapest	U.S.S.R.	Moscow
India	New Delhi	Yugoslavia	Belgrade

CURRENCIES OF VARIOUS COUNTRIES

Argentine	peso, centavo	Japan	yen
Australia	dollar, cent	Kenya	shilling, cent
Belgium	franc, centime	Mexico	peso, centavo
Canada	dollar, cent	New Zealand	dollar, cent
Chinese People's		Nigeria	naira, kobo
Republic	yuan	Poland	zloty, grosz
Denmark	krone, öre	Portugal	escudo, centavo
Egypt	pound, piastre	Republic of	
France	franc, centime	South Africa	rand
Germany	Deutsche Mark	Spain	peseta, céntimo
Greece	drachma, lepton	Switzerland	franc
Holland	guilder, cent	Turkey	lira, juru
India	rupee, paisa	United States	dollar, cent
Italy	lira, centesimo	U.S.S.R.	rouble, kopeck

DO YOU KNOW:

1. With which **country or people** each of the following is associated?

Ali	Foreign Legion	Midnight Sun	scimitar
Alphonse	Fritz	moccasins	shamrock
Balmoral	furs	Mounties	sombrero
Beefeater	Hans	mummies	stiletto
beret	heather	onions	tea
bolas	ice-cream	oranges	thistle
boomerang	John Bull	ostrich	tigers
butter	kangaroo	reindeer	tomahawk
cheese	kilt	rickshaw	tulips
chop-sticks	lariat	Rising Sun	turban
chrysanthemum	leek	rose	Uncle Sam
clogs	lotus flower	salmon	vodka
corn flower	macaroni	sandals	watches
daffodil	Marianne	Sandy	whisky
fez	Magyar	sari	windmills

2. With which **countries** do you associate the following beasts of burden?
    camel, dog, donkey, dromedary, elephant, horse, llama, mule, ox, reindeer, yak.

3. Who use (or used) the following kinds of boats?
    canoe, coracle, dhow, galleon, gondola, junk, kayak, sampan.

4. What **national** names are often attached to the following?
    Example: **Kenya** coffee. **Scotch** broth.
    baths, butter, cakes, carpets, cheese, drill, onions, sausage, stew, tea.

5. Who use (or used) these weapons?
    boomerang, claymore, cutlass, harpoon, tomahawk, truncheon.

6. In what **country** would you be if your journey was called a *(a)* safari, *(b)* mush, *(c)* hadj, *(d)* trek?

Useful Information

7. In which **countries** men might have each of the following names?

    Angus MacDonald, Tom Smith, Evan Jones, Patrick O'Neil, Chang Wu, Fritz Schmidt, Ivan Petrovitch, Juan Caballero, Pierre Sablon, Hans Brinker.

8. The **town and country** in which each of the following is situated?

    Cleopatra's Needle, Colosseum, Eiffel Tower, Leaning Tower, Nelson's Monument, Pyramids, The Golden Gate, The Golden Horn, The Houses of Parliament, The Kremlin, The Pool, The Statue of Liberty, The Sphinx, The Taj Mahal, The Bridge of Sighs, The White House, The Vatican.

9. In which **countries** the following mountains are situated?

    Ben Nevis, Mt. Etna, Mt. Everest, Fujiyama, Mt. Blanc, Snowdon, Table Mountain, The Rockies, Uhuru Peak, Vesuvius.

10. With which **countries** the following famous people are associated?

    Bonnie Prince Charlie, Buffalo Bill, Captain Cook, De Valera, General Franco, General Wolfe, George Washington, Gandhi, Haile Selassie, Joan of Arc, Jomo Kenyatta, Julius Caesar, Mussolini, Napoleon, Nelson, Peter the Great, Queen Victoria, Robert the Bruce, Roosevelt, The Kaiser, The Mikado, Wellington, William Tell, Stalin, Churchill, Wilberforce.

11. To what **countries** the following names (seen on foreign stamps) apply?

    Argentina, Belgique, Danmark, Eire, Suomi, France, Deutschland, Nederland, Italia, Norge, Polska, Romania, España, Sverige, Suisse or Helvetia.

THE WONDERS OF THE WORLD

In olden times travellers who visited foreign lands generally brought back amazing tales of the wonderful sights they had seen on their journeys. The most famous of these sights became known as the Seven Wonders.

1. The Pyramids of Egypt.
2. The Hanging Gardens of Babylon.
3. The Tomb of Mausolus at Halicarnassus.

4.   The Temple of Artemis (Diana) at Ephesus.
5.   The Colossus at Rhodes.
6.   The Statue of Zeus (Jupiter) at Olympia.
7.   The Pharos Lighthouse at Alexandria.

Of the above **Seven Wonders of the Ancient World** only the Great Pyramids of Egypt survive today.

In the Middle Ages people considered that there existed other sights quite as wonderful and named the following:
1.   The Colosseum of Rome.
2.   The Leaning Tower of Pisa.
3.   The Catacombs of Alexandria.
4.   The Great Wall of China.
5.   Stonehenge.
6.   The Porcelain Tower of Nanking.
7.   The Mosque of St. Sophia in Constantinople (Istanbul).

All of these **Wonders of the Middle Ages** (some of which are much older than the Middle Ages) still stand or have remains which can still be seen.

Today it would be impossible to make a completely satisfactory list of Seven Wonders as we have all seen or heard of many amazing man-made structures and scientific marvels. Under these two headings the following are remarkable enough to be included in any list of **Wonders of the Modern World:**

Man-made Structures
1.   Simplon Tunnel.
2.   The Sky-scrapers of New York (U.S.A.).
3.   The Boulder Dam of Colorado (U.S.A.).
4.   The Panama Canal (Central America).
5.   The Golden Gate Bridge at San Francisco (U.S.A.).
6.   The Taj Mahal at Agra (India).
7.   North Sea Oil drilling rigs and production platforms.

Scientific Marvels

1. Internal Combustion Engine.	2. Concorde.
3. Space Travel.	4. Anaesthetics.
5. Heart Surgery.	6. Bio-engineering.
7. Radio.	8. Radar.
9. Fibre-optics communication.	10. Television.
11. Lasers.	12. Computers.

Useful Information

1.	doctor's "listening" instrument	stethoscope
2.	magnifies tiny objects	microscope
3.	makes distant objects look bigger, nearer	telescope
4.	measures heat and cold	thermometer
5.	measures heat of the body	clinical thermometer
6.	indicates the weather	barometer
7.	measures gas or electricity used	meter
8.	helps the voice to carry	megaphone
9.	picks up sound for sending out again	microphone
10.	carries messages by wire	telephone
11.	carries sound without use of wires	radio
12.	carries messages by wire across the sea	cable
13.	takes photographs	camera
14.	takes photographs through the body	X-rays
15.	glasses used for bettering the eyesight	spectacles
16.	pocket instrument used for telling time	watch
17.	tells if a thing is horizontal	spirit-level
18.	tells if a thing is vertical	plumb-line
19.	gives direction	compass
20.	a sailor's map	chart
21.	a ship which can travel below the water	submarine
22.	attracts iron	magnet
23.	makes electricity	dynamo
24.	ship's engine which works by steam	turbine
25.	a machine for measuring time	clock
26.	measures angles in surveying	theodolite
27.	instrument for drawing circles	compasses
28.	releases over-pressure of steam	safety-valve
29.	machine used in business for letter-writing	typewriter
30.	causes the spark in motor engine	magneto/distributor

Sound travels 1·6 km in 5 seconds.

Light travels approximately 300,000 km in 1 second.

Light takes 8 minutes to reach the Earth from the Sun.

36 km per hour is equal to 10 m per second.

1 litre of water weighs 1 kg.

1 nautical mile is 1·85 km.

Home
attic
bolster
cellar
chimney
curtains
cushion
detergent
hearth
kitchen
lobby
mattress
meter
mirror
parlour
pillow
poker
saucer
scullery
towel
tumbler

Clothing
braid
cloak
costume
cotton
flannel
gabardine
garments
jacket
linen
lingerie
muslin
petticoat
satin
stocking
trousers
tweed
velour
velvet
waistcoat
woollen

People
adult
ancestors
aunt
babies
children
comrade
cousin
friend
guest
hostess
maiden
nephew
niece
orphan
parents
relation
uncle
visitor
widower
youth

Trades
butcher
carpenter
chemist
clothier
doctor
draper
druggist
engineer
grocer
journalist
lawyer
mason
mechanic
plumber
purveyor
riveter
sawyer
sculptor
tailor
wright

Body
ankles
arteries
exercise
forehead
heart
knees
knuckles
limbs
lungs
muscles
nostrils
shoulder
skeleton
skull
stomach
thigh
throat
tongue
veins
wrist

Travel (1)
aeroplane
airship
balloon
bicycle
brakes
carriage
coach
cruise
electricity
engine
express
fares
gangway
guard
label
locomotive
luggage
machine
omnibus
parcel

Food
bacon
biscuits
bread
butter
cheese
chocolate
cocoa
coffee
margarine
marmalade
mutton
porridge
pudding
sago
salmon
sandwich
sausages
steak
sugar
venison

Travel (2)
passengers
pedals
pier
platform
purser
saloon
seaplane
signal
skis
sledge
sleigh
steerage
steward
tourist
tramway
traveller
tunnel
vehicle
wagons
whistles

Spelling Lists

Land	Sea	Sky	Coast
cape	billows	altitude	bathing
cliff	breakers	astronomy	beach
continent	breakwater	atmosphere	billows
country	channel	cloudy	breeze
headland	crest	comet	cliffs
hillock	fiord	creation	cockles
island	harbour	crescent	costume
marsh	inlet	dawn	diving
mound	lagoon	eclipse	herring
mountain	lake	hazy	lobster
pampas	loch	heavens	mussels
peninsula	ocean	horizon	pier
plain	river	midnight	rowing
prairie	rivulet	planet	seaweed
precipice	sea	solar	shingle
summit	streamlet	sunset	swimmer
tundra	torrent	telescope	view
valley	tributary	twilight	whelks
veldt	trough	universe	winkles
volcano	waves	zenith	wreck

Time	Sport	School	Hospital
ancient	badminton	calendar	accident
annual	bowls	ceiling	casualty
August	boxing	chalk	chloroform
autumn	cricket	composition	disease
century	fencing	copies	doctor
Christmas	football	cupboard	fever
dawn	golf	dictation	infection
Easter	hockey	easel	massage
era	polo	grammar	medicine
February	putting	history	ointment
gloaming	release	hymns	operation
January	rounders	interval	paralysis
minutes	rugby	partition	physician
modern	shinty	pastels	plaster
punctual	skating	pencil	poison
Saturday	sleighing	picture	sterilize
September	sprinting	poetry	surgeon
Thursday	tennis	pupil	thermometer
Tuesday	wrestling	scholar	tonic
Wednesday	yachting	teacher	ward

Animals (1)
ape
armadillo
badger
bat
bear
beaver
buffalo
bull
camel
cat
cow
deer
dog
donkey
dromedary
elephant
ferret
fox
gazelle
giraffe

Animals (2)
goat
gorilla
hare
hedgehog
hippopotamus
horse
hyena
jackass
jaguar
kangaroo
leopard
lion
llama
lynx
mole
mongoose
monkey
moose
mouse
mule

Animals (3)
otter
ox
panther
pig
porcupine
puma
rabbit
rat
reindeer
seal
sheep
skunk
squirrel
stoat
tiger
walrus
weasel
whale
yak
zebra

Dogs
Airedale
Alsatian
bloodhound
bulldog
borzoi
collie
dachshund
Dalmatian
greyhound
Newfoundland
Pekinese
pointer
Pomeranian
poodle
retriever
Saint Bernard
setter
sheepdog
spaniel
terrier

Birds (1)
albatross
blackbird
budgerigar
canary
chaffinch
cormorant
corncrake
crane
crow
cuckoo
curlew
dipper
duck
eagle
falcon
finch
flamingo
gannet
goose
guillemot

Birds (2)
hawk
heron
jackdaw
kingfisher
lapwing
magpie
moorhen
nightingale
owl
oyster-catcher
parrot
partridge
peewit
pelican
penguin
pheasant
pigeon
plover
puffin
raven

Birds (3)
redshank
robin
rook
sandpiper
seagull
skylark
snipe
sparrow
starling
stork
swallow
swan
swift
tern
thrush
turkey
vulture
wagtail
woodpecker
wren

Fish
cod
dogfish
eel
flounder
flying-fish
goldfish
haddock
halibut
herring
mackerel
pike
plaice
roach
salmon
shark
skate
sole
swordfish
trout
whiting

Spelling Lists

Trees	Flowers (1)	Flowers (2)	Insects
apple	aster	lotus	ant
ash	bluebell	lupin	bee
beech	buttercup	marigold	beetle
birch	carnation	narcissus	bug
cedar	chrysanthemum	orchid	butterfly
chestnut	crocus	pansy	centipede
elm	daffodil	peony	cricket
fir	dahlia	poppy	daddy-long-legs
hawthorn	daisy	primrose	dragonfly
larch	dandelion	queen-of-the-meadow	earwig
lime	forget-me-not	rhododendron	flea
maple	foxglove	rose	fly
oak	geranium	snowdrop	gnat
olive	gladiolus	sunflower	grasshopper
palm	honeysuckle	sweet pea	locust
pine	hyacinth	thistle	louse
poplar	iris	tulip	midge
rowan	lilac	violet	mosquito
sycamore	lily	wall-flower	moth
yew	lily-of-the-valley	water-lily	wasp

Fruit	Vegetables	Minerals	Liquids
apple	bean	aluminium	acid
apricot	beetroot	brass	alcohol
banana	cabbage	bronze	beer
blackcurrant	carrot	coal	brine
bramble	cauliflower	copper	cider
cherry	celery	gold	cocoa
currant	cucumber	granite	coffee
damson	garlic	iron	lemonade
gooseberry	leek	lead	milk
grape	lettuce	marble	oil
lemon	onion	mercury	paraffin
melon	parsley	nickel	petrol
orange	parsnip	platinum	port
peach	pea	radium	sherry
pear	potato	silver	tea
pineapple	radish	slate	turpentine
plum	rhubarb	steel	vinegar
raspberry	sprout	sulphur	water
strawberry	tomato	tin	whisky
tomato	turnip	zinc	wine

TEST 1

1. Give the general analysis of:

> When the girl returned from **London** she told **her** father **that** she had seen a **grizzly** bear which **performed** tricks in the circus.

2. Parse the words printed in **bold** type in Question 1.

3. *(a)* State the feminine of:

   instructor, bachelor, horse, manservant, husband.

   (b) Give the plural of:

   knife, child, penny, sheep, piano.

4. Insert the names of the creatures:

   The .... brays.   The .... hoots.
   The .... grunts.   The .... chatters.
   The .... croaks.   The .... bleats.
   The .... barks.   The .... neighs.
   The .... howls.   The .... trumpets.

5. Correct the following sentences:

   (1) He said that you done it.
   (2) She is the biggest of the twins.
   (3) It was me that took the pencil.
   (4) The man went for to get the book.
   (5) A piano was sold to the lady with carved legs.

TEST 2

1. Select from each of the following sentences the subordinate clause and tell its kind and relation:

   (a) The cottage where Burns was born stands **near** Ayr.
   (b) He told **me secretly** where he was going.
   (c) The **soldiers** slept where they found a **resting** place.

2. Parse the words printed in **bold** type in Question 1.

General Tests

3.   Supply the missing words:

      Example: As sharp as a needle.

As black as ....   As fast as ....

As meek as ....   As happy as ....

As brave as ....   As keen as ....

As sweet as ....   As steady as ....

As cold as ....   As fit as ....

4.   *(a)*   Give the objective case of:

      I, he, you, we, they.

    (b)   Give the past tense of:

      does, hides, writes, sings, bites.

5.   Change the **bold** type clauses into phrases:

(1)   The child was in bed **before the sun had set**.

(2)   Flowers will grow **where conditions are suitable**.

(3)   Remember to write **when you arrive**.

(4)   I saw her **when the clock struck four**.

(5)   I am convinced **that he is sincere**.

TEST 3

1.   Give the general analysis of:

When the gentleman arrived at his home he **discovered** that he had left **his** umbrella in the **train**.

2.   Parse the words printed in **bold** type in Question 1.

3.   Write down the Comparatives and Superlatives of:

many, hot, evil, famous, little.

4.   *(a)*   Name the homes of the following:

tinker, hare, gipsy, eagle, bee.

    (b)   By adding a prefix form words opposite in meaning to:

possible, secure, welcome, use, legal.

5.   Change all Singulars into Plurals and Verbs into Past Tense:

(1)   The rabbit runs from the dog.

(2)   The girl wears a blue dress.

(3)   The sailor swims to his ship.

(4)   He has a sharp knife.

(5)   I keep my bird in a cage.

TEST 4

1. Read the following sentence and then answer the questions below:

   When I heard that the man was seriously injured I resolved to help him in every way possible.

   (a) Write out the adverbial clause.

   (b) What parts of speech are: I, seriously, resolved, possible?

   (c) What part of the verb is **"to help"**?

   (d) What number is **him**?

   (e) What is the subject of **was injured**?

   (f) Write down the preposition in the sentence.

2. (1) Form nouns from:

   introduce, loyal, revive, ready, broad.

   (2) Form adjectives from:

   parent, reason, fortune, poet, winter.

3. Use any five of the following words (one for each sentence) to form short sentences:

   instinct, obstinate, traditional, respectively, occurrence, standard, respectable, resolved.

4. Put the correct prepositions in the blank spaces:

   (1) The boy was told not to meddle .... the pencils.

   (2) She felt ashamed .... herself.

   (3) The man took great pride .... his garden.

   (4) The child has been lost .... Thursday.

   (5) He hurried home .... school.

5. What is meant by saying a person is:

   (a) hard up,   *(f)* at rest,

   (b) hard of hearing,   *(g)* lion-hearted,

   (c) stuck up,   *(h)* ill-used,

   (d) dead beat,   *(i)* an old salt,

   (e) all ears,   *(j)* out of sorts?

General Tests

1. Give the general analysis of the following sentence:

    We were **thoroughly** alarmed when information reached us that the **train** in **which** our friends were travelling had been involved in a **serious** accident.

2. Parse the words printed in **bold** type in Question 1.

3. *(a)* Some Christian names have popular short names, e.g.
    Robert — Bob, Catherine — Kate.
    Give the short names for:
    Albert, Christina, Frederick, Patrick, Elizabeth.

    (b) In which countries do the following peoples live?
    Dutch, Hindus, Eskimos, Greeks, Welsh.

4. Punctuate and insert capital letters where necessary:

    do you think said my friend in a whisper that theres a chance of escape certainly i replied.

5. Insert the following phrases in their sentences:

    rack and ruin, thick and thin, head and shoulders, safe and sound, out and out.

    (a) The ship reached harbour ....
    (b) The man was an .... rascal.
    (c) She is .... taller than her brother.
    (d) Later through foolishness he went to ....
    (e) The soldiers would follow their general through ....

TEST 6

1. Read the following sentence and then answer the questions below:

    When the man reached the garden gate he noticed that the old house in which he was born was in ruins.

    (a) What parts of speech are:
    garden, that, which, was, ruins?

    (b) Write out the principal clause.

    (c) Write out the subordinate adjective clause.

    (d) Name kind of sentence.

2. In the following list of words, one word seems out of place. Underline the word you consider is wrong:

> Coat, hat, gloves, curtains, stockings.
> Blue, yellow, ruler, green, pink.
> Saw, envelope, plane, hammer, chisel.
> Anchor, rope, string, twine, cord.
> Needle, pin, scissors, thimble, spoon.

3. Where would you look to find:

> The address of a person?
> The position of a place?
> The meaning of a word?
> The day and date of the month?
> Something which happened the previous day?

4. Give the past tense and past participle of the following verbs:

> break, fly, hide, ring, swim.

5. What is meant in each of the following proverbs?

> *(a)* Let sleeping dogs lie.
> *(b)* Too many cooks spoil the broth.
> *(c)* Once bitten twice shy.

TEST 7

1. Add a clause and name the kind of clause you add:

> *(a)* We ran for shelter ....
> *(b)* When the rain stopped ....
> *(c)* Mary told him ....
> *(d)* The cunning fox .... could not be caught.

2. Correct the following sentences:

> *(a)* Walk as quick as possible.
> *(b)* He has forgot the address.
> *(c)* Neither Tom or I can swim.
> *(d)* This end of the rope is the thickest.
> *(e)* The time was $\frac{1}{4}$ past 9.

General Tests

3.   Make a noun from **strong**.

Make a verb from **courage**.

Make an adjective from **obey**.

Give the opposite of **poverty**.

Give a similar word to **mute**.

4.   Medal, board, loose, waist, hoping, lose, meddle, hopping, bored, waste.

Fill in the blank spaces of the following sentences, using the most suitable words from the above list:

The teacher told the little boy not to .... with the .... as it had a .... hinge. The child went over to the .... paper box .... to find his pencil.

5.   The following is written in the **singular number** and **present tense**. Change it into **plural number** and **past tense**.

I have a cousin who stays on that little farm. He knows that I like to come here on my holiday.

TEST 8

1.   Read the following sentence carefully and then answer the questions below.

When the soldiers reached the city walls they saw that the town which the enemy had completely ruined had been deserted for some time.

(a)   Give the case and relation of: town, which, walls.

(b)   What parts of speech are: city, that, reached, enemy, for, some?

(c)   Write out the subordinate adverbial clause.

2.   (1)   Give the opposites of:

seldom, visible, praise, export, advance.

(2)   Give similar words to:

enemy, purchase, feeble, perceive, conceal.

3. Your answer in each case should be one word:

  (a) A person who collects fares.

  (b) Water which has turned into gas.

  (c) Name of metal container for oil.

  (d) A place where birds are kept.

  (e) Conveys sick or injured to hospital.

4. Join the following ten words in pairs so that they form five sensible compound words:

  head, black, gentle, dust, egg, bin, ache, board, cup, man.

5. *(a)* Complete these proverbs:

  (1) A stitch in time ....

  (2) A bird in the hand ....

  (3) Birds of a feather ....

  (4) A rolling stone ....

  (5) First come ....

  (b) Give the meaning of:

  a.m., Co., B.B.C., G.P.O., p.m., M.P., U.K., A.D., U.S.A., J.P.

TEST 9

1. Add a clause and name the kind of clause you add:

  (a) The boys ran away ....

  (b) The lady .... was my sister.

  (c) The man saw .... when he returned.

  (d) .... before the child arrived.

2. State the masculine of:

  witch, duck, aunt, vixen, wife.

  Give the singular of:

  loaves, armies, roofs, sheep, feet.

General Tests

3. Use each of these verbs — frowned, mumbled, sang, chuckled, bowed, whispered, listened, smiled — once only to complete the following sentences:

(1) He .... tunefully.

(2) He .... angrily.

(3) He .... humbly.

(4) He .... indistinctly.

(5) He .... gleefully.

(6) He .... broadly.

(7) He .... attentively.

(8) He .... softly.

4. A number of sheep together is called a **flock**.

What name is given to a number of:

ships, insects, herring, angels, thieves, wolves, chickens, savages, pups, players?

5. Make each pair of sentences into one sentence without using **and** or **but** or **so**.

(a) The house was destroyed. It was built by Tom's father.

(b) He works hard at his lesson. He wishes to succeed.

(c) The men were walking quickly. The men saw me.

(d) He heard the strains of music. He was passing the church.

(e) The lady lost the book. She was going to the library.

TEST 10

1. Read the sentences below and then answer the questions:

Our little hut was situated among the high mountains near the river Dee. Along the banks lay green pastures to which deer came frequently in winter.

(a) What case is **hut**?

(b) What kind of noun is **Dee**?

(c) What part of speech is **our**?

(d) Parse **among**.

(e) What is the subject of **lay**?

(f) Parse **frequently**.

(g) What tense is **came**?

(h) What part of speech is **which**?

(i) What gender is **deer**?

(j) What part of speech is **high**?

2. (1) Form adjectives from: affection, nature, attraction, pride, value.

(2) State opposites of: success, arrive, often, sense, entrance.

3. Make sentences, one for each word, showing the correct use of:

coarse, course, root, route, rode, rowed, currant, current, hoard, horde.

4. Rewrite the following correctly:

a boy said to his chum where are you going james oh replied the other i'm on my way home.

5. Give one word in place of each:

(a) A fertile place in the desert.
(b) A person who by desire lives alone.
(c) An instrument for measuring heat and cold.
(d) A person who looks on the bright side of things.
(e) A stream which flows into a river.

TEST 11

1. *(a)* Make a sentence containing **that he would come** as a noun clause.

(b) Make a sentence containing **which he bought** as an adjective clause.

(c) Make a sentence containing **when he reached the station** as an adverbial clause.

2. Give the plural of **ox**.
Give the feminine of **tiger**.
Word for a young **swan**.
The home of an **Eskimo**.
Adverb from **danger**.

3. Put in the suitable words in the spaces below:

Example: **Little** is to **Big** as **Dwarf** is to **Giant.**
Sheep is to **Mutton** as **Pig** is to ....
High is to **Low** as .... is to **Down.**
Soldier is to .... as **Sailor** is to **Navy.**
.... is to **Herring** as **School** is to **Whales.**
Bee is to **Hive** as **Cow** is to ....

General Tests

4. Change the following **Complex Sentences** into **Simple Sentences**:

(1) There is a boy who is very proud.

(2) He spoke to me while he was passing.

(3) The girl who is intelligent gave the right answer.

(4) The man bought a boat which is very big.

(5) We received word that he was rescued.

5. With which countries do you associate the following famous people?

Robert the Bruce	George Washington ....
Stalin	Napoleon ....
Captain Cook	De Valera ....
David Livingstone............	Jomo Kenyatta ....
Lloyd George	Gandhi ....

TEST 12

1. Read the sentence and then answer the questions below:

When the boys who were playing in the park heard the school bell ringing loudly they were afraid that they would be late.

What parts of speech are:
who, park, loudly, school, that?

What part of the verb is **playing**?

What is the case of **bell**?

What is the number of **boys**?

What is the subject of **heard**?

What is the gender of **they**?

2. *(a)* Give the gender of:
lion, cousin, jotter, waitress, friend.

(b) Give words similar in meaning to:
lair, disappear, inside, empty, quickly.

3. Give the names of the shops where you would buy the following:

fruit	....	spectacles	....	flowers	....
hats	....	milk	....	newspapers	....
fish	....	meat	....	sweets	....
tobacco	....				

4. Change all nouns and verbs into plural:

    (1) The lady is very beautiful.   (4) The valley is broad.

    (2) Is the salmon fresh?   (5) The goose makes a loud noise.

    (3) The son-in-law is ill.

5. Who use the following articles?

hoe	....	anvil	....	spanner	....
solder	....	palette	....	safety-lamp	....
awl	....	"goose"	....	hod	....
cleaver	....				

TEST 13

1. In the following sentences there are groups of two words within brackets. One of the two words is correct, the other wrong. Underline the correct word:

    (1) William can (ran, run) faster than (I, me).

    (2) It was (me, I) who (did, done) it.

    (3) George and (he, him) (has, have) gone on holiday.

    (4) Between you and (me, I) I think they (was, were) wrong.

    (5) (He, Him) and (me, I) are twelve years of age.

2. A number of sheep is called a flock. Insert the most suitable word in each of the following:

    (1) a .... of wolves   (5) a .... of ships

    (2) a .... of bees   (6) a .... of singers

    (3) a .... of herring   (7) a .... of thieves

    (4) a .... of cattle   (8) a .... of savages

General Tests

3. In the following sentences underline the correct word of the two words within brackets:
   (1) You ought to visit her now (but, that) you know where she stays.
   (2) Write down the answers (as, when) you were taught.
   (3) The boy tried hard (but, that) he failed.
   (4) (Than, When) he comes let us know.
   (5) The man was careful (except, lest) he should fall.

4. (a) Give the plural of:
   deer, mouse, pansy, tooth, woman.

   (b) Give the masculine of:
   cow, duchess, duck, waitress, niece.

5. By accident the sentences of this story were jumbled. Re-arrange them in their proper order:
   Fortunately he saved her from serious injury.
   Suddenly her ball rolled into the middle of the road, and she ran after it.
   A passer-by saw the girl's danger and ran to her aid.
   A little girl was playing on a busy street.
   At that moment a motor came dashing round the corner.

TEST 14

1. In the following sentences underline the correct word of the two words within brackets:
   (1) How he managed it remains a (duty, mystery).
   (2) James was honest and (deceptive, diligent).
   (3) The stranger asked if I could (direct, inform) him to the station.
   (4) The (remedy, illness) or cure is very simple.
   (5) His opinion differed (against, from) mine.

2. (a) Punctuate the following correctly:
   tell me said the old gentleman what is your name.

   (b) Form adjectives from:
   reason, success, south, fool, France.

156

3. Use the correct prepositions in the blank spaces:

(1) The bottle was filled .... water.
(2) He was told not to meddle .... the toys.
(3) The two brothers divided the apple .... them.
(4) That hat is similar .... mine.
(5) I hope I can rely .... you.

4. With whom do you associate the following?
       Example: anvil — blacksmith.

(1)	rifle	....	(5)	letters	....
(2)	prescription	....	(6)	pulpit	....
(3)	telescope	....	(7)	sheep	....
(4)	spectacles	....	(8)	joy-stick	....

5. Opposite each phrase are groups of words in brackets. Underline the group of words in brackets which gives the correct meaning of the phrase:

       down in the mouth (speaking quickly) (in low spirits)
       a peppery individual (a quick-tempered person) (a happy person)
       out of sorts (not well) (of great courage)
       hard up (good enough) (short of money)
       beside oneself (annoyed and angry) (nothing to do)

TEST 15

1. *(a)* Underline the correct word of the words in brackets:

       A man who writes stories is an (artist, author, sculptor).
       A bed on board ship is called a (bunk, cabin, saloon).
       A person who hoards money is a (martyr, miser, cashier).
       A vessel for holding flowers is a (caddy, scuttle, vase).
       The flesh of a cow is called (beef, mutton, pork).

(b) Underline the group of words in brackets which gives the correct meaning of the phrase:

       to play the game (to act fairly) (to run quickly)
       to bury the hatchet (to chop wood) (to make peace)
       to cut a dash (to hurt one's leg) (to be very showy)
       to smell a rat (to be suspicious) (to hunt mice)
       to show the white feather (to be cowardly) (to capture an Indian)

General Tests

2. Underline the correct word of the two words in brackets:
   (a) Sam as well as George (was, were) at the circus.
   All of you but Tom (has, have) the wrong answer.
   A purse containing three coins (was, were) found.
   One and all (is, are) going to the concert.
   Neither the one nor the other (is, are) right.

   (b) His friend and (he, him) travelled to Paris.
   Was it (I, me) you saw there?
   Between you and (I, me) I am sure he is wrong.
   Fred is younger than (I, me).
   Let you and (I, me) hide.

3. (a) Willie has (grew, grown) very tall.
   The town crier (rang, rung) his bell.
   The boy (began, begun) to look for his pencil.
   Has he (wrote, written) to his cousin?
   The lion (sprung, sprang) at the timid deer.

   (b) The girl wept (bitterly, faintly).
   The boy fell (clearly, heavily).
   The man crept (harshly, stealthily).
   The lady waited (patiently, deeply).
   My friend sprang (quickly, plainly).

4. (a) He neither reads (or, nor) writes well.
   (Now, When) we arrived we searched for our luggage.
   Charles is stronger (as, than) I am.
   I know (that, before) Tom is a good scholar.
   I could not pay him (that, for) I had no money.

   (b) The hunter went in pursuit (to, of) the animal.
   He suffers (from, of) a swollen head.
   I was sorry to part (of, with) that picture.
   The girl complained (with, of) a sore foot.
   The man disagreed (of, with) him.

5. (a) In the following lists of words, one word in each list is out of place. Underline this word.
   copper, lead, tin, earth, silver.
   rain, cold, snow, sleet, hail.
   corn, rye, barley, wheat, raisins.
   ear, nose, mouth, knee, chin.
   linen, leather, silk, cotton, wool.

(b) Underline the word of the same kind as the first three words in each line:

> river, brook, stream (mountain, tributary, island).
> sofa, chair, stool (cupboard, wardrobe, couch).
> limestone, marble, slate (granite, cement, mortar).
> sword, dagger, spear (revolver, rifle, lance).
> kitten, puppy, calf (duck, lamb, horse).

6. Underline the correct word of the two words in brackets:

(a) The ship tied up at the (key, quay).
He was not (allowed, aloud) to go.
The jacket was made of (course, coarse) cloth.
The (pail, pale) moon rose above the hills.
We picked up shells on the (beach, beech).

(b) Re-arrange the following sentences in their proper order so that they form a short story:

> This he did to the great joy of the onlookers.
> He refused to bow to the Governor's hat.
> He ordered him to shoot an apple from his son's head.
> The Governor wished to punish him for his disobedience.
> William Tell was a famous archer in Switzerland.

TEST 16

1. Underline the correct word of the group of words in brackets:

(1) A person who eats too much is a (miser, glutton, hypocrite).
(2) A lady who sells hats is a (milliner, florist, hosier).
(3) John, who is my aunt's son, is my (nephew, brother, cousin).
(4) A soldier who rides on horseback is in the (marines, cavalry, infantry).
(5) A wooden shelter made for a dog is a (byre, stable, kennel).

2. Give words opposite in meaning to:

present	....	bitter	....
entrance	....	polite	....
east	....	danger	....
guilty	....	lost	....

General Tests

3. Underline the correct word in each of the brackets:
   (Who, Whom) do you think I (saw, seen)?
   All but one (was, were) saved when the ship (sank, sunk).
   Each of the men (has, have) a right to (their, his) opinion.
   Between you and (I, me), the boys (wasn't, weren't) pleased.
   Let Tom and (me, I) stay after the others have (gone, went).

4. We say "As black as coal". Supply the missing words in the following:

as blind as	....	as cold as	....
as quiet as	....	as good as	....
as gentle as	....	as sharp as	....
as happy as	....	as fresh as	....

5. Following are five sentences, which, if arranged properly, would make a short story. Re-arrange them in proper order:
   The bird, highly flattered, opened her mouth to sing.
   One day a crow spied a piece of cheese on a window sill.
   The cheese fell and was soon eaten by the crafty animal.
   She picked it up and flew to a neighbouring tree.
   A cunning fox approached and praised her voice.

TEST 17

1. Christmas Day comes in the month of ....
   Flounder, herring, salmon, whiting are all ....
   The masculine of **aunt** is ....
   .... is the feminine of **hero**.
   State the plural of **tooth**.
   A number of **sheep** is called a ....
   We say "**As sharp** as a ...."
   A person who works on an **anvil** is a ....
   What animal **brays**?
   Word for a **young hen** is ....

2. Give words opposite in meaning to:
   defend, stranger, reveal, throw, compliment.

3. The noun formed from **"select"** is ....
    .... is the adjective formed from **"attract"**.
    Give a verb corresponding to **"broad"**.
    Form an adverb from **"joy"**.
    Give a compound word with **"grand"** as part of it.

4. **Bird** is to **air** as **fish** is to ....
    Table is to **wood** as **window** is to ....
    Food is to **hungry** as **drink** is to ....
    Nose is to **smell** as **tongue** is to ....
    Wrist is to **cuff** as **neck** is to ....

5. In each of the following sentences underline the correct word in brackets:
    Many of the pencils were (broke, broken).
    Everybody (was, were) pleased with the result.
    He is a little taller than (I, me).
    The man could not do (nothing, anything) to help.
    Neither the boy (or, nor) his sister will come.
    To (who, whom) do you wish to speak?
    The train moved (slow, slowly) into the station.
    The food was pleasant (for, to) the taste.
    We received a (strong, hearty) welcome.
    Water dripped from the (brim, brink) of his hat.

6. Give words similar in meaning to:
    halt, roam, margin, permit, courage.

7. Arrange the following in the correct order, beginning with **dawn**:
    dusk, noon, evening, dawn, night, morning.

8. Make short sentences, one for each word, showing the correct use of the
    following:
    their, coarse, fowl, preys, creek.

9. Give **one word** which might be used in place of the words **in bold type**:
    (a) The prices were **made less than before**.
    (b) The **people who were listening** applauded.
    (c) The little boat **turned upside down** in the storm.
    (d) The germs were **not able to be seen by the human eye**.
    (e) The missionary discovered that the natives were **people who ate
        human beings**.

10. Name **ten** different **animals**.

161

General Tests

1. The shortest month of the year is ....
   Beetroot, cauliflower, onion and parsnip are all ....
   The masculine of **wife** is ....
   .... is the feminine of **bachelor**.
   State the plural of **mouse**.
   A number of **thieves** is called a ....
   We say, "As **bold** as ...."
   A person who uses a **safety-lamp** is a ....
   What animal **neighs**?
   Word for a **young fox** is ....

2. Give words opposite in meaning to:
   arrive, sweet, fertile, legal, juvenile.

3. The noun formed from **"young"** is ....
   .... is the adjective formed from **"circle"**.
   Give a verb corresponding to **"horror"**.
   Form an adverb from **"weary"**.
   Give a compound word with **"cup"** as part of it.

4. **Walk** is to **legs** as **fly** is to ....
   Knife is to **cut** as **gun** is to ....
   Island is to **sea** as **lake** is to ....
   Statue is to **sculptor** as **book** is to ....
   Petals are to **flower** as **spokes** are to ....

5. In each of the following sentences underline the correct word in brackets:
   A tree had (fell, fallen) across the path.
   Neither Tom nor James (is, are) at school.
   She is cleverer than (I, me).
   He should (of, have) come last night.
   Either my father (or, nor) my mother will go with me.
   I saw the lad (who, whom) won the race.
   It can be done very (easy, easily).
   He had not a penny (by, to) his name.
   She has a (healthy, spotless) character.
   I divided the sweets (between, amongst) several boys.

6. Give words similar in meaning to:
   enemy, unite, concluded, guard, envy.

162

7. Arrange the following in historical order:
      aeroplane, chariot, locomotive, rocket, motor-car.

8. Make short sentences, one for each word, showing the correct use of the following:
      fourth, route, style, soled, sewing.

9. Give **one word** which might be used in place of the words **in bold type**:
    (a)   Smoking was **not allowed** in the garage.
    (b)   The motorist drove his car **slowly and carefully**.
    (c)   The boy **was very sorry for** his mean action.
    (d)   They ascended the steep steps of the **tower in which the bell was hung**.
    (e)   The castaways saw a ship on the **line where sea and sky seem to meet**.

10. Name **ten** different **birds**.

TEST 19

1. Guy Fawkes' Day is in the month of ....
    Mosquito, beetle, moth and locust are all ....
    The masculine of **niece** is ....
    .... is the feminine of **wizard**.
    State the plural of **ox**.
    A number of **pupils** is called a ....
    We say, "As **clear** as ...."
    A person who rides a **bicycle** is called a ....
    What animal **trumpets**?
    Word for a **young goat** is ....

2. Give words opposite in meaning to:
      ancient, purchased, private, rare, majority.

3. The noun formed from **"choose"** is ....
    .... is the adjective formed from **"voice"**.
    Give a verb corresponding to **"deed"**.
    Form an adverb from **"critic"**.
    Give a compound word with **"ball"** as part of it.

General Tests

4. **Picture** is to **wall** as **carpet** is to …………

Graceful is to **clumsy** as **polite** is to …………

Descend is to **depth** as **ascend** is to …………

Gas is to **pipes** as **electricity** is to …………

Castle is to **tower** as **church** is to …………

5. In each of the following sentences underline the correct word in brackets:

I have never (went, gone) by bus.

None of the pencils (is, are) missing.

He is much older than (I, me).

We were (learned, taught) how to read correctly.

The boy could neither read (or, nor) write.

(Who, Whom) do you wish to see?

How (quick, quickly) the time has passed!

We waited (upon, for) him at the station.

Between you and (I, me), someone must have taken it.

He divided the apple (between, amongst) his two brothers.

6. Give words similar in meaning to:

vacant, remedy, concealed, grief, faith.

7. Arrange the following in historical order:

canoe, submarine, coracle, steam-ship, sailing-ship.

8. Make short sentences, one for each word, showing the correct use of the following:

waste, aloud, seized, medal, site.

9. Give **one word** which might be used in place of the words **in bold type**:

(a) The boy **purposely kept out of the way of** his employer.

(b) The flowers were **not real, but made of cloth, wax and paper.**

(c) The motor-car **slipped sideways across the road.**

(d) During the fire, the birds had died from **want of air to breathe.**

(e) They managed to fix it with a **sticky substance obtained from the hoofs of animals.**

10. Name **ten** different **flowers**.

TEST 20

1. We live in the .... century.
   Coal, iron, slate and lead are all ....
   The masculine of **nun** is ....
   .... is the feminine of **colt**.
   State the plural of **deer**.
   A number of **singers** is called a ....
   We say, "As **keen** as ....".
   A person who uses a **palette** is an ....
   What animal **howls**?
   Word for a **young hare** is ....

2. Give words opposite in meaning to:
   enemy, success, expand, miser, exposed.

3. The noun formed from **"receive"** is ....
   .... is the adjective formed from **"bible"**.
   Give a verb corresponding to **"grass"**.
   Form an adverb from **"ability"**.
   Give a compound word with **"stone"** as part of it.

4. **Sheep** is to **flock** as **tree** is to ....
   Banana is to **peel** as **egg** is to ....
   Speak is to **shout** as **walk** is to ....
   When is to **time** as **where** is to ....
   Lawyer is to **client** as **doctor** is to ....

5. In each of the following sentences underline the correct word in brackets:
   The boy had (rose, risen) at eight o'clock.
   Every one of us (has, have) an equal chance.
   My sister is five years younger than (I, me).
   Do try (to, and) come on time.
   Neither a borrower (or, nor) a lender be.
   (Who, Whom) do you think we met?
   I managed not so (bad, badly).
   They were impatient (from, at) the delay.
   That is a (trivial, trifling) excuse.
   Let Tom and (I, me) go.

General Tests

6. Give words similar in meaning to:

commence, repair, odour, prohibited, renown.

7. Arrange the following in historical order:

oil-lamp, firebrand, electricity, candle, gas.

8. Make short sentences, one for each word, showing the correct use of the following:

groan, rays, rowed, cruise, cereal.

9. Give **one word** which might be used in place of the words **in bold type**:
- *(a)* The runner was completely **tired and worn out** after the race.
- *(b)* The injured man was **unaware of anything that was going on around him.**
- *(c)* The rude girl continually **broke into** her parents' conversation.
- *(d)* He **changed his appearance by dressing** himself as a native.
- *(e)* The story caused **a state of excited feeling.**

10. Name **ten** different **fruits**.

TESTS IN COMPREHENSION

TEST 1

Read the following passage carefully and then answer the questions below:

THE STORY OF A GREAT RIVER

From its source in the mountains between Sierra Leone and Guinea to its delta in Eastern Nigeria the mighty Niger will have travelled some 4,000 kilometres. This nine-month-long journey to the far-off Gulf of Guinea will take it through many countries and some of the most varied scenery in the world.

From the high mountains around Futa Jallon through the dense forests of Guinea it flows, gaining in size from its many tributaries. Its waters create the fertile plains of the Mali Republic before reaching the desert regions beyond Timbuktu whence it turns south-eastwards to flow between the republics of Niger and Benin.

It is here that it enters Nigeria, that great African state and, more than half its journey over, is put to work. Vast hydro-electric plants provide for the needs of Nigeria's millions and for the industry of this huge country. Here, too, irrigation schemes, fed by its waters, assist in food production and its use, with specially designed vessels, to facilitate travel, trade and the transport of goods. And everywhere there are fishermen casting their nets.

At Lokoja, where the Niger is joined by its greatest tributary, the Benue, it turns sharply southwards to flow majestically past Onitsha and presently to form its vast delta. This delta, hot and humid, is a place of great rain forests, mangrove swamps and a network of waterways taking the Niger at last to the sea. Here, too, and in the sea offshore, are the oil-fields which make Nigeria one of the main oil producers of the Commonwealth of Nations.

		Marks
1.	Where is the source of the Niger?	(1)
2.	Name four towns on its banks.	(2)
3.	Through which countries does it pass?	(1)
4.	In which country is its delta?	(1)
5.	In your own words describe a delta.	(3)
6.	In your own words describe a mangrove.	(2)
7.	What is opposite in direction to south-east?	(2)
8.	What confluence occurs at Lokoja?	(2)
9.	Find out and write about Mungo Park.	(5)
10.	Write short notes on the following: Hausa, Yoruba, Ibo, Fulani, Tiv, Kanuri.	(6)
		25

Tests in Comprehension

TEST 2

Read the following passage carefully and then answer the questions below:

HOMEWORK INTERRUPTED

Tabu looked up from his book, in a lazy way at first, to see what had made the noise. Then he went stiff with fright. At an arm's length away from his chair, something moved. A shape glided smoothly along the window frame. He saw a flat head held up by a slender neck. A puff adder!

The snake stopped and lay without moving. It looked dead. But all the time it was trying to sense if any food was in the room.

Tabu felt trapped in his chair, yet he knew he must warn his sister. He thought of what his father had told him so often. He wanted to whisper, but his mouth and tongue were dry with shock. He dared not move. His throat clicked as he tried to utter some sound. If only she would look at him!

Masya must have felt that there was something strange about his silence, for she turned her head to glance at him. When she saw the fear on his face, she swiftly shifted round, looking at his glazed eyes. She moved her head to see what those eyes were fixed on, then covered her mouth to stifle her gasp of terror.

(From *World Wide Adventure Series* Reader 5 — published by Robert Gibson.)

		Marks
1.	What had the snake come for?	(1)
2.	Why would it stop and lie without moving?	(1)
3.	What made Tabu feel trapped in his chair?	(2)
4.	What effects did Tabu's fear have on him?	(2)
5.	Why would he wish to warn his sister?	(2)
6.	What do you think Tabu's father had told him so often?	(2)
7.	What caused Masya to look at Tabu?	(1)
8.	How did she come to see where the danger was?	(1)
9.	Why did she cover her mouth?	(2)
10.	What might have happened if Tabu had moved?	(2)
11.	What do you think Tabu wanted to warn his sister to do or not to do?	(4)
12.	What would you have done in Tabu's place?	(5)

25

TEST 3

Read the following passage carefully and then answer the questions below:

THE FOX

The fox is probably the most intelligent of all quadrupeds. It is allied to the dog and closely resembles the Alsatian, the wolf, the hyena, the coyote (prairie-wolf of North America), the dingo (native dog of Australia), and the dhole (wild dog of India). Its chief points of difference from the others are the sharper muzzle and the shorter legs in proportion to the size of the body. Its tail or "brush" is also longer, and its ears more erect.

The fox has eyes which contract in strong light and expand in darkness. This enables the animal to hunt at night. It excavates its own lair by burrowing much like a rabbit, but frequently it is a thief in this respect as it steals burrows from other animals and converts them into its own "earth". The cunning and slyness of the animal is shown by the number of exits to its lair. As many as ten bolt-holes from the fox's "earth" have been counted. Its power of scent is very acute, and its hearing very highly developed. The animal has a peculiar strong scent, which leaves the "trail" in the so-called sport of fox-hunting. When the chase is keen Reynard frequently escapes by dashing into wide and open drain-pipes. For this reason one may see gratings placed over the mouths of many road-side and field drains. When cornered by the hounds the animal has been known to climb roofs of houses and to dash into nearby cottages in desperate efforts to shake off its pursuers.

		Marks
1.	What is a quadruped?	(1)
2.	Name ten animals mentioned in the passage.	(5)
3.	Give four points of difference between the fox and the dog.	(4)
4.	Why is the fox able to hunt at night?	(1)
5.	Name any other creature which hunts at night.	(1)
6.	What two words are used for the fox's den?	(2)
7.	Of what use are bolt-holes?	(1)
8.	What animal does the fox resemble when digging?	(1)
9.	Give two reasons why the fox is a difficult animal to catch.	(2)
10.	What enables the hounds to track down the fox?	(1)
11.	What special name is sometimes given to a fox?	(1)
12.	According to the passage, why do gratings sometimes cover drain-pipes?	(1)
13.	What is meant by "When the chase is keen"?	(1)
14.	Give the meanings of the following words as used in the passage: contract, excavates, frequently, converts, scent, peculiar.	(3)

$$\frac{}{\underset{=\!=}{25}}$$

Tests in Comprehension

Read the following passage (supposed to have been written by a boy) and then answer the questions below:

> When I had finished breakfast the squire gave me a note addressed to John Silver, at the sign of the Spy-glass, and told me I should easily find the place by following the line of the docks, and keeping a bright look-out for a little tavern with a large brass telescope for sign. I set off, overjoyed at this opportunity to see some more of the ships and seamen, and picked my way among a great crowd of people and carts and bales, for the dock was now at its busiest, until I found the tavern in question. It was a bright enough little place of entertainment. The sign was newly painted; the windows had neat red curtains; the floor was newly sanded. There was a street on either side, and an open door on both, which made the large, low room pretty clear to see in, in spite of clouds of tobacco smoke. The customers were mostly sea-faring men; and they talked so loudly that I hung at the door, almost afraid to enter. As I was waiting, a man came out of a side room, and, at a glance, I was sure he must be Long John. His left leg was cut off close by the hip, and under the left shoulder he carried a crutch, which he managed with wonderful dexterity. He seemed in the most cheerful spirits, whistling as he moved about among the tables.

		Marks
1.	To whom was the squire's note addressed?	(1)
2.	Where was this person to be found?	(1)
3.	At what time of day did the boy set out?	(1)
4.	What route was he to take?	(1)
5.	Why was the boy overjoyed?	(2)
6.	When the boy had found the tavern in question, what did he notice about *(a)* the sign, *(b)* the windows, *(c)* the floor?	(3)
7.	Who were the customers?	(1)
8.	Why was the boy almost afraid to enter?	(2)
9.	Where was John Silver when the boy first looked into the tavern?	(1)
10.	What nickname is used in the passage?	(2)
11.	Describe John Silver's unusual appearance.	(4)
12.	How do you know Silver was happy?	(1)
13.	Give another word of the same meaning for each of the following: spy-glass, tavern, opportunity, glance, dexterity.	(5)

25

TEST 5

Read the following passage carefully and then answer the questions below:

SIGHTSEEING IN SINGAPORE

You do not have to go far in Singapore to discover the unexpected or the unusual. A stroll through Chinatown could bring you face to face with a cartful of masks for people to wear to represent mythical or historical characters in a procession or an operatic or theatrical performance during some festival — heads of heroes and villains, horses and lions, unicorns and dragons, all crafted with loving care and selling at surprisingly low prices. Go and listen to the early morning "concert" of birdsong from hundreds of caged birds. Have your initials carved in semi-precious stone to make your own personal seal. Notice the old women working on a construction site, clad in black and wearing red head-dresses. These are the Samsui sisters who have voluntarily chosen to adopt this way of life and remain unmarried.

The variety of things to do in Singapore is endless. Relax on a tropical beach, take a stroll through a lush green park or visit an Indian temple. You can spend hours in the Zoological Gardens with their world-famous Orang-utan colony, spot 350 different species among the 7,000 birds in the Bird Park, see the Orchid Garden with its thousands of blooms that would cost a king's ransom in London, or visit a crocodile farm.

After your sightseeing you may be hungry, and there is no better place to be hungry than in Singapore. Rich aromas will draw you to one of Singapore's 8,000 open-air food-stalls offering Chinese, Malay, and Indian dishes in all their infinite variety — with a banana leaf, perhaps, to serve as your plate and end the day with yet another surprise.

		Marks
1.	What is a *mythical* character?	(2)
2.	How is a *historical* character different?	(2)
3.	How do *operatic* and *theatrical* productions differ?	(2)
4.	What does *crafted* mean? Why is it a good word here?	(2)
5.	Why would the low prices be surprising?	(2)
6.	Why is the word "concert" in inverted commas?	(2)
7.	What would be the purpose of having a personal seal?	(2)
8.	What is a construction site?	(2)
9.	What does the word *species* mean? What is its singular?	(2)
10.	What does *a king's ransom* mean and why?	(2)
11.	What would be the purpose of a crocodile farm?	(2)
12.	Distinguish *flavours, aromas, smells* and *perfumes*.	(3)

25

(Information Source: Singapore Tourist Promotion Board.)

Tests in Comprehension

TEST 6

Read the following passage carefully and then answer the questions below:

THE LONG TREK

Steve reckoned that they were about three miles from the river, if there was still a river. By now, it might be just a trickle of slow-moving water, or a bed of dried mud, full of tumbleweed and stones.

He closed his eyes to slits as he peered through the clouds of dust — red dust kicked up by hundreds of hoofs. The cattle that streamed past him as he sat slumped in his saddle were as tired and worn out as the exhausted men who drove them.

Some of them bellowed with fear and pain. The calves pushed their noses into the sides of the cows that had no more milk to feed them. All of them were mad with thirst and very thin. From their knob-like backbones, the drawn skin was tight over the fleshless haunches. Their ribs curved like the bars of a cage over their sunken flanks. They were starving.

They had trekked from the cattle stations in the north of Australia where usually heavy rains filled streams and pools. But this was a year of drought. The burning sun, which had sucked up the last drops of water, had left the ground cracked and dry. Wide, dangerous ruts had formed in the earth. They were deep and broad enough to wedge a man's boot when he walked. There was only one thing to do. The cattle must be driven many miles south, to the river; or they would die.

(From *World Wide Adventure Series* Reader 5 — published by Robert Gibson.)

		Marks
1.	Why did Steve sit "slumped" in his saddle?	(2)
2.	What did he fear might have happened to the river?	(3)
3.	Why were the animals' backbones like knobs?	(1)
4.	What other effects had the drought had on them?	(3)
5.	What is a drought?	(1)
6.	Why would the ground have cracks?	(2)
7.	Had the sun really "sucked" up drops of water?	(3)
8.	Why were the ruts in the earth dangerous?	(1)
9.	If the river was dry, what then?	(4)
10.	What effects would a drought have in your area?	(5)

$$\underline{\underline{25}}$$

TEST 7

Read over the following passage and then answer the questions below:

THE DEATH OF JAMES I OF SCOTLAND

The king, while he was staying at Perth, took up his residence in the abbey of Black Friars, there being no convenient palace in the town, and this made it easier for his enemies to carry out their purpose, as his guards and officers were staying in different houses.

Just as James, having dismissed all his attendants, was preparing to go to bed, the Highland woman who had already warned him at the ferry again demanded permission to speak with the king, but was refused on account of the lateness of the hour. Suddenly a clashing of armour was heard in the garden and flashes of light from torches were thrown against the windows. The king, hearing the voice of Sir Robert Graham, his deadly enemy, guessed that the intruders had come to murder him. He called to the ladies to keep the door as well as they could, while he tried to get out at the windows, but the bars would not budge. By the help of tongs, however, he lifted a plank of the flooring, and let himself down into a narrow vault beneath. This vault had formerly had an opening into the courtyard of the convent, by which he might have made his escape, but the unfortunate James forgot that, only three days before, he had caused the opening to be built up, because when he played at ball in the courtyard the ball used to roll into the vault through that hole.

The queen and her women endeavoured as well as they might to keep the door shut, and one of them, Katherine Douglas, boldly thrust her arm across the door in place of the bar, which the conspirators had removed the day before.

Marks

1. Why did the king stay in an abbey at Perth? (1)
2. Why did the king's enemies find it easy to attack him in the abbey? (1)
3. Why did the woman want to speak with the king? (2)
4. Why was the Highland woman turned from the door? (1)
5. What two things alarmed the king and the ladies? (2)
6. Why did the king fear the intruders? (2)
7. Why could James not jump from a window? (1)
8. How did the king escape from the room? (1)
9. When the king let himself into the vault what did he expect to do? (2)
10. Why had the vault entrance been closed? (2)
11. How had the conspirators prepared, the day before, for the murder? (2)
12. Describe a "torch" of the time of this story. (2)
13. Give another word with the same meaning for each of the following: residence, convenient, budge, unfortunate, endeavoured, conspirators. (6)

$$\frac{}{25}$$

Tests in Comprehension

TEST 8

Read this passage carefully and then answer the questions below:

SHIPWRECK ON A CORAL ISLAND

A huge wave snatched up the oar that we had decided to cling to instead of joining the ship's crowded boat, and . . .

I came to on the shore to find young Peterkin trying to staunch the flow of blood from my badly cut brow, and learned from Jack that we appeared to be the only survivors, alone on an uninhabited island.

It soon occurred to Peterkin, the youngest of us at fourteen, that hunger and thirst might be a problem. The ship's stores were sunk in deep water. What would we do? Jack pointed up to the branched head of a coconut palm. "There, look!" he said, "Nuts at all stages."

In no time Peterkin had monkeyed up and tossed down three nuts about the size of a football.

"Let's visit the wreck first," said Jack, "and then eat."

Though only eighteen himself, Jack was our natural leader and no-one objected, Peterkin comforting himself by telling us that he'd rather find a spring, and have a drink, than eat.

"Then hop up that tree again," said Jack, "and throw down another nut, a green one this time, unripe."

Surprised, but always game, Peterkin did as he was told.

"Now cut a hole in it with your knife and clap it to your mouth."

Peterkin did as directed, and we both burst into uncontrolled laughter at the changes that instantly passed over his face. No sooner had he put the nut to his mouth and thrown back his head to catch what came out, than his eyes opened to twice their ordinary size, while his throat moved vigorously in the act of swallowing. Then a look of intense delight spread over his face — except, of course, his mouth, which was otherwise engaged. At length he stopped, drew a long breath, and exclaimed, "Nectar! Perfect nectar!"

		Marks
1.	What happened between the first and second paragraphs?	(2)
2.	How are we expected to know this?	(2)
3.	Why is *staunch* a better word than *stop* (paragraph 2)?	(2)
4.	What did Jack mean by "nuts at all stages"?	(2)
5.	What do the words *monkeyed* and *hop* suggest?	(2)
6.	Why could they not get food from the wreck?	(2)
7.	Why did Jack first speak of eating but not drinking?	(2)
8.	What sentences show Jack as a good leader?	(2)
9.	Is *objecting* different from *refusing*?	(2)
10.	Why did the others laugh at Peterkin?	(2)
11.	What feelings can make us wide-eyed?	(2)
12.	What does "otherwise engaged" mean?	(1)
13.	What was the point of exclaiming "Nectar!"?	(2)

25

TEST 9

Read this passage carefully and then answer the questions below:

NATURE AND THE TRAVELLER IN THE CARIBBEAN

Nature shows off to the traveller in the Caribbean. Start in the Cayman Islands and she introduces you to some of her prize travellers, the turtles that swim thousands of miles to these sandy shores to lay their eggs.

Watch Neptune's gliders, the "flying" fish, skimming the tips of waves as you make for Jamaica and sail into one of the world's great natural harbours. Go ashore and see huge crawling monsters clawing out mountains of bauxite from which will come aluminium, "silver from clay", to be made into kitchen utensils and tomorrow's jumbo jets.

Don't miss seeing the phenomenal lush growth of a tropical rain-forest, on Dominica, where the tree canopy blots out the sun.

On Barbados stand and watch the Atlantic's majestic rollers crashing against the foot of the island's northern rock-face, tossing up spray twice the height of the cliffs. There too you will marvel, as elsewhere, at the unimaginable number of tiny coral insects that had to live and die to form these miles of bright clean sands, reefs and whole coral islands.

Drive over the wild moon landscape of the crater of St. Lucia's Soufrière volcano, its deafening jets of steam showing it is not yet dead, only sleeping. Then take your pictures, as everyone does, of the island's twin sugar-loaf mountains rising 800 metres sheer out of the sea, and move on, perhaps flying over the volcanoes of St. Vincent and Granada, their craters now occupied by lakes, to busy Trinidad. Here see the pitch lake Sir Walter Raleigh used to waterproof his ships' hulls, and which today, after four hundred years, still supplies asphalt for our roads.

And these ships in the bay? Nature will fill them again and again with the oil she has made from the remains of living things that lived here long before history.

Now step over to South America and see one final marvel, Guyana's Kaieteur Falls, five times the height of Niagara, a spectacular end to an unforgettable trip.

Marks

1.	Does nature "show off"? What is meant?	(2)
2.	In what two ways are the turtles "prize travellers"?	(2)
3.	Does the writer think flying fish really fly?	(2)
4.	What "crawling monster" would you see in Jamaica?	(2)
5.	Why is aluminium called "silver from clay"?	(2)
6.	What makes the forests on Dominica so lush?	(2)
7.	Compare *rollers* with other words that could be used.	(2)
8.	How are coral reefs formed?	(2)
9.	What do the words *moon landscape* suggest?	(2)
10.	Is it better to call the volcano *sleeping* than *dormant*?	(2)
11.	Explain the second last paragraph.	(3)
12.	What makes things *spectacular*?	(2)

25

Tests in Comprehension

TEST 10

Read this passage carefully and then answer the questions below:

MONDAY MORNING

Monday morning found Tom Sawyer miserable. Monday morning always found him so, because it began another week's slow suffering in school. He generally began that day with wishing he had had no intervening holiday; it made the going into captivity and fetters again so much more odious.

Tom lay thinking. Presently it occurred to him that he wished he was sick; then he could stay at home from school. Here was a vague possibility. He canvassed his system. No ailment was found, and he investigated again. This time he thought he could detect colicky symptoms, and he began to encourage them with considerable hope. But they soon grew feeble and presently died wholly away. He reflected further. Suddenly he discovered something. One of his upper teeth was loose. This was lucky; he was about to groan, as a "starter", as he called it, when it occurred to him that if he came into court with that argument his aunt would pull it out, and that would hurt. So he thought he would hold the tooth in reserve for the present, and seek further. Nothing offered for some little time, and then he remembered hearing the doctor tell about a certain thing that laid up a patient for two or three weeks and threatened to make him lose a finger. So the boy eagerly drew his sore toe from under the sheet and held it up for inspection. But now he did not know the necessary symptoms. However, it seemed well worthwhile to chance it, so he fell to groaning with considerable spirit.

Mark Twain

		Marks
1.	Where was Tom when he was doing his thinking?	(1)
2.	What prospect was making him miserable?	(1)
3.	What made the misery worse on Mondays?	(1)
4.	What was the purpose of his thinking?	(1)
5.	What three ideas did he have for achieving his purpose?	(3)
6.	What caused him to reject his first idea?	(1)
7.	How do we know he thought the second idea was better?	(1)
8.	Why did he not adopt this second idea?	(1)
9.	How did he set about carrying out his third plan?	(1)
10.	What weakness can you see in this third plan?	(1)
11.	In what sense was Tom facing captivity and fetters?	(1)
12.	What is meant by the words "canvass" (compare "canvas") and "system"?	(2)
13.	What would Tom do in "canvassing his system"?	(2)
14.	In the phrase "came into court with that argument" what court is meant, and what argument?	(2)
15.	What is meant by holding the tooth "in reserve"?	(1)
16.	What is the difference between a symptom and an ailment?	(2)
17.	What words used in the passage refer to *feelings*, and what other words refer to *thinking*?	(3)

25

TEST 11

Read this passage carefully and then answer the questions which follow:

Africa is the second largest continent and is a land of great contrasts. It has burning deserts and luxurious forests teeming with animal life.

North of the Sahara Desert on the Mediterranean Coast are the Arab States, to the South are the ex-colonies, now self-governing. Europe is only 9 miles from the North African coast at the Straits of Gibraltar. To the North East, in Egypt, the Suez Isthmus joins Africa to Asia. The Isthmus is cut by the 72-mile stretch of the Suez Canal which provides passage for ships from the Indian Ocean to the Mediterranean and the Atlantic.

The equator passes through the centre of Africa at Mount Kenya, and most of the continent lies in 'the tropics', i.e. between the Tropic of Cancer and the Tropic of Capricorn.

Because of Africa's smooth coastline there are few inlets and bays.

The largest island is the Malagasy Democratic Republic in the Indian Ocean. The Cape Verde Islands, the Canaries, and Madeira are all groups of islands off the North West coast.

Most of the land is one vast plateau. There is only a narrow coastal plain in most places but this broadens in the North East and North West. The plateau is stepped, and on each "step" there are wide flat tracts of land with few mountains.

One remarkable feature of the geography of the continent, and indeed of the world, is the great Rift Valley, formed where the land has sunk between two faults in the Earth's crust. One branch of this Rift is occupied by Lake Albert in Uganda, Lake Tanganyika, Lake Nyasa and the last 200 miles of the course of the Zambesi River. The other branch runs through Kenya from Lake Nyasa and is occupied by the Red Sea in the North, continuing up the Gulf of Aqaba and the valley of the river Jordan in Asia.

There are three great deserts which form two fifths of the continental area, the Sahara in the North (largest in area) the Kalahari in the South and the Namib along the South West coast.

The highest mountain is Kilimanjaro, with its 19,340 feet (5895 metres) Uhuru Peak which is always snow-covered though almost on the Equator. This and other mountains are volcanic in origin and few volcanoes are still active. The Atlas mountains cut off the Sahara from the Western Mediterranean and the Atlantic. The second largest fresh-water lake in the world, Lake Victoria, lies between the two arms of the Rift Valley.

Africa's rivers include some of the longest in the world. The Nile drains huge areas from the Equator to the Mediterranean providing Egypt with rich silt for crops and water to irrigate them. The Congo basin is one of the world's great tropical rain forests. The Niger probably waters more countries than any other river. The Zambesi boasts the world's greatest waterfalls and, like the Volta, has been put to work to provide millions with electricity.

Tests in Comprehension

1. The passage is about:
    - A. *the Sahara Desert*
    - B. *the geography of Africa*
    - C. *the African coastline*
    - D. *the Tropic of Capricorn.*
2. Which of these has nothing to do with the passage?
    - A. *the Malagasy Republic*
    - B. *drilling for oil*
    - C. *the Sahara Desert*
    - D. *the Indian Ocean.*
3. From the passage we learn:
    - A. *Africa is the second largest continent*
    - B. *Africa is a winter resort of migrant birds*
    - C. *Africa is moving slowly (drifting)*
    - D. *Africa has four deserts.*
4. According to the passage, Africa is:
    - A. *one vast plateau*
    - B. *full of deserts and mountains*
    - C. *surrounded by islands*
    - D. *made up of jungle.*
5. The Atlas Mountains
    - A. *lie beside the Mediterranean*
    - B. *meet the Indian Ocean*
    - C. *join Egypt at the Suez Canal*
    - D. *cut off the Sahara from the Western Mediterranean.*
6. From the passage we can conclude:
    - A. *Africa has a rocky coastline*
    - B. *Africa is surrounded on three sides by Oceans*
    - C. *it is possible to sail right round Africa*
    - D. *snow is unknown in Kenya.*
7. The largest island off the African Coast is:
    - A. *Madeira*
    - B. *Canaries*
    - C. *the Cape Verde Islands*
    - D. *the Malagasy Republic.*
8. There is a narrow coastal plain:
    - A. *to the North around the Atlas mountains*
    - B. *south of the Equator*
    - C. *to the south-west at the Namib desert*
    - D. *in most places.*
9. From the passage we learn that the great Rift Valley was formed by
    - A. *erosion due to weather*
    - B. *volcanic eruptions*
    - C. *sinking of the land between cracks in the earth's crust*
    - D. *rivers gouging out a channel for themselves.*
10. From the passage, which of these is not a feature of African geography?
    - A. *the Kalahari Desert*
    - B. *ships in the Suez Canal*
    - C. *the smooth coastline*
    - D. *the great plateau.*
11. Where does the Mediterranean meet the Atlantic?
    - A. *at Malagasy*
    - B. *Lake Victoria*
    - C. *at Gibraltar*
    - D. *near the Sahara Desert.*

A GOOD STANDARD ENGLISH PRONUNCIATION

Unless you pronounce your words correctly giving the vowels and consonants their correct value, the sounds which you make will not be understood. In this chapter we set out most of the variety of sounds used in speaking English, give you practice in these sounds and identify, and help you to avoid, the common errors of speech. Throughout this chapter, where further practice is considered desirable reference has been made to the lists of words in *Sounds of Words* Books 1 or 2 (published by Robert Gibson). Although the *Sounds of Words* (SOW) books were written for a much younger age group they are the most systematic and thorough Phonic books on the market.

We will start with the simple single vowel sounds and proceed by easy stages to cover and give practice in all the necessary sounds. Remember to practise the starters until you sound perfect before going on to complete words.

Some *'a'* sounds
Practise starters *ma', pa', ra', ca', fa'*.
ma'n, pa'n, ra'n, ca'n, fa'n, Dan, Sam, Pam, tan, yam.
(For further practice SOW Book 1, pages 7 & 8.)

Some *'e'* sounds
Practise starters *be', le', ke', pe', te'*.
be'g, le'g, ke'g, pe'g, Te'd, bed, led, fed, sell, fell.
(For further practice SOW Book 1, pages 11 & 12.)

Some *'i'* sounds
Practise starters *wi', ki', ti', bi'*.
wi'll, wi'n, ki'd, li'd, bi'll, lip, sip, pick, sick, wick.
(For further practice SOW Book 1, pages 15 & 16.)

Some *'o'* sounds
Practise starters *fo', no', lo', so'*.
fo'g, no'd, lo'g, no't, so'p, bog, cot, dog, for, got.
(For further practice SOW Book 1, page 19.)

Some *'u'* sounds
Practise starters *gu', bu', cu', du'*.
gu'n, gu'm, bu'n, cu't, du'll, bus, cup, fur, hurt, just.
(For further practice SOW Book 1, pages 21 & 22.)

A Good Standard English Pronunciation

Revision

it, pat, pig, us, van, mat, jug, bed, lad, met, mutt, tan, led, yam, cup, dog, Meg, hog, hug, sip.

For further revision in the sounds you have just learned, turn to SOW Book 1, page 23.

'ck'

Remember to prolong the vowel and emphasise the final *'ck'*.

Practise starters *ba', ne', ti', to', su'*.

ba'ck, ne'ck, ti'ck, to'ck, su'ck, lack, peck, sick, lock, luck.

(For further practice SOW Book 1, page 25.)

Emphasise the final consonants

damp, send, kept, pack, rust, went, sand, text, rack, pump.

(For further practice SOW Book 1, pages 27, 28, 29, 30.)

Get the 'starters' correct

bla'ck, cri'sp, sti'ck, tra'mp, sta'ck, dre'ss, dru'm, lucky, sorry, fuzzy.

(For further practice SOW Book 1, pages 32, 33, 35.)

The missing 'e'

The *'e'* is not pronounced in certain words.

candle, dazzle, paddle, fizzle, battle, cattle, kettle, puddle.

(For further practice SOW Book 1, page 39.)

The 'sh' sound

Practise the *'sh'* 'starters' *sha', she', shi', sho', shu'*.

shirt, shop, sham, shell, shed, shut, shock, shot, short, shod.

(For further practice SOW Book 1, page 41.)

Note that *'sh'* at the end of the words has the same sound.

fish, dish, crush, crash.

(For further practice SOW Book 1, page 42.)

The 'th' sound

Practise the *'th'* starters and endings.

thumb, cloth, father, mother, wrath, lath, that, thong, thing, them, bath.

(For further practice SOW Book 1, pages 43 & 44.)

The 'ch' sound

Practise the starters and endings.

chick, church, match, branch, latch, batch, chap, chip, check.

(For further practice SOW Book 1, pages 45 & 46.)

The 'wh' sound

Practise the starters *whi', wha', whe'*.

whi'p, whi'sk, whi'stle, wha't, when, where, whit, whack, whiz, whim.

(For further practice SOW Book 1, pages 47 & 48.)

A Good Standard English Pronunciation

The 'ng' sound
  wing, bang, sting, hang, sang, rang, long, rung.
  (For further practice SOW Book 1, page 50.)

a — e
  The silent 'e' changes the 'a' sound.
  The silent 'e' makes 'a' as in *man*, sound *ā* as in *day, hay, lay*.
  ba'ke, ba'se, ha're, ta'ble, case, lake, make, cake.
  (For further practice SOW Book 2, pages 4 & 5.)

i — e
  The silent 'e' changes the 'i' sound.
  The silent 'e' changes the 'i' as in *lip, pip* to 'i' as in *fire*.
  Practise starters *fi', mi', pi', li', hi'*.
  fire, mine, pipe, like, hide, dice, white.
  (For further practice SOW Book 2, pages 6 & 7.)

o — e
  The silent 'e' changes the 'o' sound as in *rod* to the 'o' as in *rode*.
  nose, toes, roes, goes, prose, floes, notes, mote, rote.
  (For further practice SOW Book 2, pages 8 & 9.)

u — e
  The silent 'e' changes the 'u' sound as in *tub, rub* to the 'u' as in *tube*.
  cube, tune, cure, use, rude, pure, glue, blue, true.

'y'
  The 'y' sounds like 'i'.
  Practise the 'y' sound — fly, sky, try, dry, fry, cry, shy, by, my.

'i'
  Practise this new 'i' sound.
  tie, die, died, cried, fried, tried, spied, shied.

'i' Another sound
  child, wild, mild, kind, hind, mind, blind, find, bind, rind.

Revision a — e, i — e, o — e, u — e, y, i.
  Remember to sound your starters and go over the sounds you have just learned. Remind yourself of the various similar 'y' and 'i' sounds.
  (For further revision SOW Book 2, pages 12 & 13.)

'ay' 'ai'
  'ay' as in *play* and *hay* sounds the same as 'ai' in *rain* and *sail*.
  tray, may, say, pail, mail, day, Kay, jay, pray, wait.
  (For further practice SOW Book 2, pages 14 & 15.)

A Good Standard English Pronunciation

'ee'

'ee' as in *see, wee, wheel, week*
seek, leek, feel, heel, keep, meet, peek, reek, seek, deer, jeer, seer.
(For further practice SOW Book 2, pages 16 & 17.)

'ea'

'ea' as in *ear* and *eat* sounds the same as the 'ee' sound.
pea, sea, lea, dear, tear, fear, gear, hear, near, rear.
(For further practice SOW Book 2, pages 18 & 19.)

'qu' = kw

'qu' as in *queen, squeak, quack.*
quads, quail, quake, quart, quench, quick, quest, quiet, quit, quiz.

'oo'

'oo' as in *soot, rook, book* requires considerable practice in the starters *roo',
boo', too', coo'.*
rook, pool, took, tool, hook, cook, nook.
(For further practice SOW Book 2, pages 22 & 23.)

'ow'   'ou'   (Two similar sounds)

'ow' as in *now*.
how, brown, bow, dower, power, row, sow, tower.
'ou' as in *out*.
flour, found, shout, ouch, sound, round.
(For further practice SOW Book 2, pages 24 & 25.)

'wa'   'aw'   'all'

'wa' as in *warm* is a similar sound to 'aw' as in *saw*: and the 'a' in *all* says 'aw'
as in *ball*.
'wa' as in *wad*.
waddle, waffle, walk, wallet, walrus, waltz, war, ward, warn, wash.
'aw' as in *awful*.
awning, awkward, bawl, dawn, dawdle, fawn, hawk, lawn.
'all' as in *tall*.
stall, ball, call, fall, gall, hall, mall, wall.
(For further practice SOW Book 2, pages 26 & 27.)

'oa'

The 'oa' sound is that of a long 'o' as in *loaf*.
goat, goal, oak, soak, oar, oats, boat, coat, coast, foam, goal, hoax.
(For further practice SOW Book 2, pages 28 & 29.)

A Good Standard English Pronunciation

'ow'

The *'ow'* sound, usually at the end of a word, is that of a long *'o'* as in *slow*.
below, arrow, sparrow, barrow, harrow, narrow, stow, row, crow, throw, lower, snow.
(For further practice SOW Book 2, pages 30 & 31.)

'ce' = s

The *'ce'* sound is that of *'s'* as in *mice*.
lace, voice, face, choice, dice, cedar, cease, dance, lance, glance.
(For further practice SOW Book 2, pages 32 & 33.)

'ge' = j

The *'ge'* sound is that of *'j'* as in *rage*.
cage, hinge, gem, gender, general, gentle, sage, savage, lunge, manage, strange.
(For further practice SOW Book 2, page 34.)

Revision

Go back to the *'ai'*, *'ay'* sounds and, doing a few starters, say aloud five of each sound up to *'ge'*.
(Further revision SOW Book 2, page 35.)

The silent 'k'

'k' before *'n'* is silent as in *knot*.
knee, knife, knock, kneel, knot, knob, know, knoll, knell.
(For further practice SOW Book 2, page 36.)

The silent 'w'

'w' before *'r'* is silent as in *wreck*.
wrong, wrap, write, wretch, wren, writhe, wrath, wring, wristlet, wrench, wrestle.
(For further practice SOW Book 2, page 37.)

The silent 'b'

lamb, thumb, dumb, numb, crumb, bomb, comb, climb.
(For further practice SOW Book 2, page 38.)

The silent 't'

whistle, castle, wrestle, bustle, rustle, listen, often, soften, glisten, hustle.
(For further practice SOW Book 2, page 38.)

SPELLING GUIDE

ADVICE

Remember the appearance of difficult words you meet in books.

Your mind's eye is a great aid to good spelling and will often tell you what is right (or wrong).

Consult your dictionary if in any doubt.

Pronounce words correctly when you speak. For example:

Pronounce the *r* after the *b* in *February*.

Pronounce the *g* in *recognise*.

Pronounce *secretary* as four syllables, and so on.

Your ear will then help you to avoid many mistakes.

Though English spelling refuses to be bound by rules, some rules are worth studying for the help they can give.

i BEFORE *e*, EXCEPT AFTER *c*

The rule is only partly true, but can be improved thus:

'If sounded as *ee*, then *i* before *e*, except after *c*.
If they sound *ay* or *eye*, then *e* before *i*.'

This table shows the variety of cases:

Spelling	Sounded as:	Examples and Exceptions
ie	*ee* in *see*	belief, cashier, chief, hygiene, grieve, siege. *Exceptions:* protein, seize, weir, weird, and personal names like Neil, Reith, Sheila.
ie	*i* in *bit*	sieve, mischief, mischievous, handkerchief. *Exceptions:* foreign, forfeit, surfeit.
ei	*ee* in *see* (after *c*)	ceiling, conceive, deceit, perceive, receipt. *Exceptions:* specie, species (and see below).
ei	*ay* in *day*	eight, neighbour, reign, sovereign, weigh.
ei	*ey* in *eye*	eiderdown, either, height, neither, sleight.
ei	*e* in *met*	heifer, leisure. *Exceptions:* friend, lieutenant.
i + e	separate	diet, glazier, soviet, science.
e + i	separate	deity, homogeneity.

Note: ie is found after *c* where *ci* sounds *sh* in:
ancient, conscience, deficient, efficient, proficient, sufficient.

PLURALS OF NOUNS

English nouns have a great variety of plural forms — one result of inheriting and borrowing from many languages:

–s   added to the singular — by far the most common form.
        bats, bones, days, keys, chiefs, pianos.

–es added to the singular where the singular ends in *–s* or another sibilant (hiss) sound, *–ss*, *–x*, *–sh*, *–ch*.
        asses, lynxes, wishes, torches, lunches.

–s   is added to most singulars ending in *–o* but *–es* to some, and either *–s* or *–es* to others.

    –s for Italian, Spanish, art, musical terms, abbreviations
        pianos, altos, sopranos, sombreros, photos.

    –s for singulars ending in two vowels
        shampoos, studios, patios, kangaroos, videos.

    –es buffaloes, dominoes, mosquitoes, tomatoes, volcanoes.

    –s or *–es* flamingo(e)s, motto(e)s, stiletto(e)s.

–ies replaces *–y*, but NOT *–ay*, *–ey*, *–oy*, or *–uy* of singulars.
        allies, berries, copies, hobbies, tries, varieties.

–ves replaces *–f* or *–fe* of the singular in a few words.
        elves, shelves, sheaves, wives.

–x   is added to the singular — beaux, bureaux (from French).

–i   replaces *–us* as in fungus, fungi; radius, radii (Latin).

–a   replaces *–um* as in stratum, strata; datum, data (Latin).

–ices replaces *–ex* as in index, indices (Latin).

–es replaces *–is* as in axis, axes; basis, bases (Greek).

–a   replaces *–on* as in criteria, phenomena (Greek).

    See also page 6 for plurals formed by changing a vowel, nouns with two plurals, plurals the same as singulars, nouns which have no singular, and for further examples.

Spelling Guide

SPELLING WORDS WITH SUFFIXES

We add suffixes to words for a variety of purposes — for example, to make plurals, to make adjectives from nouns, adverbs from adjectives, etc. See pages 6, 76 to 78, 122, 124.

Quite often the spelling of a base word is changed when a suffix is added. In almost every case it is the last letter of the base word that is affected.

For example:

Final *y* becomes *i*	easy+ly becomes easily.
Final *e* is dropped	hope+ing becomes hoping.
Final consonant doubled	hop+ing becomes hopping.

Final –*y*

Final –*y* after consonants usually becomes *i* (*ie* before *s*)
deny, denie-s, deni-ed, deni-al; luxury, luxurious;
beauty, beautiful; marry, marriage; sixty, sixtieth.

Exceptions: 1.   Keep the *y* before –*ing*, and –*ist*
drying, replying, copying, copyist.
2.   shyly, shyness, slyly, slyness, dryness, beauteous (but dryly or drily).
3.   people's names: as in "the Kellys".

Following a vowel, final *y* is normally kept
pay, payable, payment; prey, preys, preyed; boys, boyish; joyful, joyous; buyer, buying.

Exceptions: paid, unpaid, laid, mislaid, said, slain, daily, gaily, gaiety.

Make a list of these words, close your book, and write correctly spelt new words formed from them by adding the suffix shown:

buoy, comply, defy, delay, display, flay, fry, imply, mortify, multiply, play, ply, pray, prey, pry, relay, reply, spray (+ *ed*).

ally, buoy, buy, comply, defy, obey, ply, replay, reply, vary (+ *ing*).

busy, dirty, fussy, grey, multiply, pray, pretty, silly, worry (+ *er*).

deny, duty, envy, fry, justify, pity, play, ply, rely, vary (+ *able*).

betray, deny, try (+ *al*); glory, joy, luxury, penury, victory (+ *ous*).

carry, marry (+ *age*); ally, comply, dally, defy, vary (+ *ance*).

Silent –e

KEEP the –e   before a suffix that begins with a consonant
love, loves, lovely; hate, hateful; safe, safety.

Exceptions: argue,   argument;   awe,   awful;   due,   duly;
nine, ninth; true, truly; whole, wholly.

DROP the –e   before a suffix that begins with a vowel
ic(e)+ed = iced; ow(e)+ing = owing;
haze, hazy; ache, aching; desire, desirous; mature, maturity.

Exceptions:

KEEP the –e where the base word ends in –ce or –ge **and** the suffix
begins with a or o
this keeps the c or g soft before the a or o
e.g. noticeable, manageable, courageous.

KEEP the –e when adding –ing
if the base word ends in –ee, –oe or –ye
e.g. seeing, agreeing, decreeing, hoeing, shoeing,
canoeing, eyeing, queueing
(but NOT in pursue, pursuing; ensue, ensuing).

KEEP the –e in dye, singe, tinge
this distinguishes   dyeing   singeing
from   dying   singing.

CHANGE the –e to i when adding –al, –ous
to certain base words ending in –ce
caprice   race   grace   vice
capricious   racial   gracious   vicious.

Make lists of these words, close your book, and write correctly spelt new
words formed from them by adding the suffix shown:

agree, argue, become, die, dine, dye, judge, menace, page, pierce, pursue,
queue, separate, serve, shoe, slope, sue, write (+ *ing*).

caprice, fame, grieve, nerve, outrage, prestige, space (+ *ous*).

believe, bridge, change, conceive, defence, deplore, desire, excuse, like,
peace, remove, reverse, service (+ *able* or *ible*).

bare, complete, due, separate, sole, sparse, true, whole (+ *ly*).

approve, dispose, peruse, race, refuse, remove, reverse (+ *al*).

coincide, cohere, contrive, ignore, emerge, guide, resemble, revere, solve,
subside, urge (+ *ance*, or + *ence*, or + *ency*).

187

Spelling Guide

Final Consonant — When to DOUBLE it, and when NOT to.

The *p* in *hop* is doubled, when *–ing* is added, to make *hopping*. Yet the *m* in *seem* is not doubled in the word *seeming*.

The difference is that in *hop* the *p* has only ONE vowel in front of it, while in *seem* the *m* has TWO.

The *r* in *confer* is doubled in *conferring*, yet the *r* in *offer* is not doubled in the word *offering*.

The difference is that, in *conferring*, the *r* is in the STRESSED syllable of the word, while in *offered* the *r* is in an unstressed syllable.

The rule that governs these differences is:

DOUBLE the final consonant of the base word if

1. it is a single consonant, and
2. there is only a SINGLE vowel in front of it, and
3. the suffix to be added begins with a vowel, and,
4. (where the base word has TWO or more syllables), the final syllable of the base word is the syllable that is stressed in pronouncing the *new* word.

Examples:

SINGLE syllable base words:

bag, bagg–age; beg, begg–ar; fat, fatt–est; red, redd–ish; madd–en, robb–ed, scrapp–ing; sinn–er, spott–ed, witt–y.

LONGER base words (stressed syllable in bold type):

be**gin**	oc**cur**	for**bid**	for**get**
be**ginn**–er	oc**curr**–ed	for**bidd**–en	for**gett**–able
be**ginn**–ing	oc**curr**–ence	for**bidd**–ing	for**gett**–ing.

Note the effect of the position of the stress in:

con**fer**	de**fer**	pre**fer**	per**mitt**–ed
con**ferr**–ing	de**ferr**–ing	pre**ferr**–ing	e**licit**–ed
confer–ence	**defer**–ent	pre**fer**–able	**bene**fit–ed.
al**lott**ed	ac**quitt**ed	e**quipp**ing	for**gett**able
balloted	**lim**ited	**gall**oping	**mark**etable.

Note that both **transfer**able and transfer**ri**ble are correct, and base words ending in *–our* drop the *u* before *–ous*, but not before *–able*:

glamour, glamorous; humour, humorous; honour, honourable.

Exceptions:

1. The final *–s* is not doubled in *gas–es*, but is doubled in *gass–ing*, *gass–ify*.

2. When the suffix *–ic* is added, final consonants are not doubled: atomic, acidic, botanic, poetic, systemic.

3. A final *–c* is not doubled, but when a suffix beginning with *e* or *i* is added to the words *mimic*, *picnic*, *traffic*, the c is supplemented with a '*k*' to keep the hard sound of the *c*:

     mimicked, picnickers, trafficking.

4. A final *w*, *x* or *y* is never doubled, e.g. saw–ing, tax–ation.

5. Where *–l* is the final consonant, the stress rule is ignored, and final *–l* is doubled in unstressed syllables, e.g.

     quarrelled, towelling, travellers, libellous, revelling.

   Exceptions: paralleled, parallelogram, scandalous, and DO NOT double final *–l* before *–ise*, *–ism*, *–ist*, *–ity*, *–ize*, e.g. civil–ise, evangel–ist, formal–ity, imperial–ist, real–ism
   (but due*ll*ist and meda*ll*ist do double the *–l*).

6. The words *kidnap*, *handicap* and *worship* do not follow the stress rule either, and the final *–p* is doubled in unstressed syllables in these words:

     kidnapped, kidnapper; handicapped, handicapping; worshipper, worshipping.

Say why the final consonant of the base word is not doubled in the following cases:

   act–or, sail–or, bow–ing, toil–ing, loud–ness, neat–est, reveal–ed, refrain–ing, exceed–ed, instal–ment, derail–ed.

Make a list of these words, close your book, and write correctly spelt new words formed from them by adding the suffix shown:

   develop, garden, jewel, murder, picnic, propel, traffic, scan (+ *er*).

   comb, envelop, favour, parallel, quit, remit, snub, trim (+ *ed*).

   envelop, expel, handicap, instal, mimic, reveal, worship (+ *ing*).

   covet, danger, glamour, humour, libel, marvel, pomp, scandal (+ *ous*).

   actual, civil, moral (+ *ity*); humour, journal, medal, novel (+ *ist*).

   bear, favour, honour, prefer, sever, suffer, suit, transfer (+ *able*).

Spelling Guide

SAME SOUND — DIFFERENT SPELLING

Words

The English language includes many pairs and trios of words which sound the same but are spelt differently. See pages 61, 62 for over a hundred examples. One simply has to learn which word is spelt which way, using a dictionary if necessary.

Licence and *practice* (nouns) are often confused with *license* and *practise* (verbs), and *prophecy* (noun) with *prophesy* (verb). Remember the difference is the same as between *advice* (noun) and *advise* (verb): your ear will tell you the verbs have the *s*.

Be sure you do not confuse these spellings:

they're	short for "they are"	*it's*	short for "it is"
their	belonging to them	*its*	belonging to it
there	in that place		(no apostrophe)
you're	short for "you are"	*who's*	short for "who is"
your	belonging to you	*whose*	belonging to whom
no	the opposite of yes	*NOES*	those voting NO
know	be aware	*nose*	part of the face

Syllables

The syllables *–cede, –ceed* and *–sede* are often confused. It helps to remember that *supersede* is the only word with the *–sede* spelling; *exceed, proceed* and *succeed* are the only words with the *–ceed* spelling. All the rest — *concede, precede, recede*, etc. — have the *–cede* spelling.

Mistakes are often made with the endings *–cal* and *–cle*. The adjectives end in *–cal* and the nouns in *–cle*. Remember one of the *nouns* (names for *things*) is *article*. Some of the adjectives are: *clerical, magical, musical, physical, practical*. Some of the nouns are *article, bicycle, circle, obstacle, spectacle, vehicle*.

Similarly *principal* (ending in *–al*) is the adjective and *principle* the noun. (*Principal* is a noun when it is used of the head of a college, but it obtained this meaning only because of its adjectival sense, the Principal being the *top* member of staff).

Vowel Sounds

The following list shows how a single individual vowel sound may be spelt in a dozen different ways:

Sound of	As in	Examples of other spellings of the same sound
a	bat	h<u>a</u>ve, s<u>a</u>lmon
a	bath	<u>au</u>nt, h<u>ea</u>rt, cl<u>er</u>k, baz<u>aa</u>r, p<u>a</u>lm, hurr<u>ah</u>
a	bathe	n<u>a</u>tion, t<u>ai</u>l, pr<u>ay</u>, camp<u>aig</u>n, str<u>aig</u>ht, b<u>ea</u>r, r<u>ei</u>ns, th<u>ey</u>, r<u>eig</u>n, w<u>eig</u>h, th<u>ere</u>, g<u>ao</u>l, g<u>au</u>ge, <u>eh</u>, d<u>a</u>hlia
e	bet	h<u>ea</u>d, s<u>ai</u>d, s<u>ay</u>s, l<u>eo</u>pard, l<u>ei</u>sure, <u>a</u>ny, R<u>ey</u>nard, fr<u>ie</u>nd, Th<u>a</u>mes, b<u>u</u>ry
e	me	th<u>e</u>me, s<u>ee</u>n, <u>ea</u>ch, f<u>ie</u>ld, s<u>ei</u>ze, k<u>ey</u>, C<u>ae</u>sar, pol<u>i</u>ce, q<u>uay</u>, p<u>eo</u>ple, B<u>eau</u>champ, <u>Oe</u>dipus
i	bit	pr<u>e</u>tty, b<u>ui</u>ld, w<u>o</u>men, br<u>ee</u>ches, s<u>ie</u>ve, g<u>i</u>ve, l<u>y</u>ric, b<u>u</u>sy
i	idle	m<u>i</u>ne, s<u>ig</u>n, h<u>ig</u>h, h<u>eig</u>ht, d<u>ie</u>, <u>i</u>sland, <u>ai</u>sle, <u>eye</u>, tr<u>y</u>, ind<u>i</u>ct, l<u>y</u>re, d<u>ye</u>, ch<u>oi</u>r
o	cot	sh<u>o</u>ne, w<u>a</u>nt, l<u>au</u>rel, kn<u>o</u>wledge, y<u>a</u>cht, h<u>ou</u>gh
au	haul	l<u>aw</u>, t<u>a</u>ll, t<u>a</u>lk, <u>ou</u>ght, <u>au</u>ght, br<u>oa</u>d, V<u>au</u>ghan
o	hero	foll<u>ow</u>, her<u>oe</u>s, follow<u>e</u>d, furl<u>ough</u>
o	note	b<u>o</u>th, t<u>oa</u>d, t<u>oe</u>, d<u>ough</u>, m<u>ow</u>, br<u>oo</u>ch, <u>oh</u>, y<u>eo</u>man, s<u>ew</u>, C<u>o</u>ckburn
oo	foot	c<u>ou</u>ld, w<u>o</u>lf
oo	fool	t<u>o</u>mb, sh<u>oe</u>, m<u>o</u>ve, s<u>ou</u>p, thr<u>ough</u>, tr<u>u</u>th, j<u>ui</u>ce, r<u>u</u>de, bl<u>ue</u>, sl<u>eu</u>th, sl<u>ew</u>, man<u>oeu</u>vre
u	shut	bl<u>oo</u>d, s<u>o</u>n, c<u>o</u>me, t<u>ou</u>ch, d<u>oe</u>s
u	duke	d<u>u</u>ty, d<u>ue</u>, s<u>ui</u>t, f<u>ew</u>, f<u>eu</u>d, l<u>ie</u>u, v<u>iew</u>, imp<u>ug</u>n, <u>ewe</u>, <u>you</u>, <u>yew</u>, man<u>oeu</u>vre, p<u>ui</u>sne
oi	coin	b<u>oy</u>, b<u>uoy</u>, c<u>oig</u>n
ou	loud	d<u>ow</u>n, b<u>ow</u>ed, b<u>ough</u>, McL<u>eo</u>d
any *vowel*	unstressed syllables	capac<u>i</u>ty, Sar<u>ah</u>, beach<u>es</u>, guin<u>ea</u>, forf<u>ei</u>t, terri<u>er</u>, hurri<u>ed</u>, tort<u>oi</u>se, c<u>o</u>mmand, Eur<u>o</u>pe, thor<u>ough</u>ly, cupb<u>oa</u>rd, hum<u>ou</u>r, hurr<u>ah</u>, pleas<u>ure</u>, b<u>u</u>ry, monk<u>ey</u>.
	before an *r*	h<u>er</u>, h<u>ea</u>rd, b<u>i</u>rd, st<u>i</u>rred, w<u>o</u>rd, col<u>o</u>nel, b<u>u</u>rst, bl<u>u</u>rred.

PHRASAL VERBS

Component Parts

Many phrases consisting of a verb and either an adverb or a preposition have meanings of their own not easily deduced from the separate meanings of the two words used in the phrase. Thus we use the phrase *to give up* in the sense of *to cease*, e.g. "I must *give up* smoking", without intending any idea of *giving* or *upward* direction.

In some cases the meaning of at least one of the words used is still apparent in the meaning of the phrase, e.g. "I shall *write up* a full account", where the word *write* still means what it says, but the word *up* means *completely*.

In some cases the same phrase may have two meanings, e.g. "You *take on* (i.e. undertake) too much." "Don't *take on* so (i.e. take offence so easily)."

Sometimes a phrase of this kind is simply metaphorical, e.g. "I confessed because I was *leant on*" (i.e. subjected to threats).

Some such phrasal verbs may include more than one adverb or preposition, e.g. "I can't *put up with* (i.e. suffer) this noise."

Some verbs, especially one-syllable verbs, are used in this way with a great variety of adverb or preposition particles, as they are called.

EXERCISES

1. Write sentences using each of these verbs with the adverb particle *up* in such a way as to show the meaning of the phrase as a phrasal verb.

    back, bring, buck, do, get, give, lay, let, look, make, put, set, turn.

2. Write sentences showing the meaning of the phrasal verbs formed by adding the particles shown to the following verbs:

    break — *down, into, off, out*
    bring — *about, in, off, on, round, to*
    call — *off, on, out*
    carry — *off, on, out*
    come — *about, across, by, in for, into, of, off, round, to, upon*
    do — *away with, down, for, in, out of, without*
    get — *about, around, at, on, on to, over, up to*
    give — *away, in, out, over*

    go — *against, ahead, along with, at, by, for, on, on about, over, with*
    keep — *back, in with, on, on at*
    knock — *about, back, down, off*
    lay — *in, into, off, on*
    look — *after, out*
    make — *for, off, out, up for*
    put — *off, on, out, up with*
    set — *in, off, out*
    stand — *by, for, in, out, up for*
    take — *after, in, off, on, to, up*
    turn — *down, in, on, out, to*